COIN COLLECTING

BIBLE

Unlock the Secrets to Building a Valuable Coin

Collection - Master Identification, Valuation,

and Preservation While Dodging Scams

- Gilbert Swanson-

Table of Contents

Book 9: Advanced Topics in   Numismatics
112

Book 1: Introduction to Coin Collecting

Coin collecting is often described as a journey, a pursuit that blends history, artistry, and the thrill of discovery. For many, the allure begins with a simple coin—perhaps a shiny penny found on the sidewalk or a curious foreign coin tucked away in a drawer. These moments ignite a passion that can lead to a lifelong hobby, filled with stories waiting to be uncovered. As you embark on this adventure, it's essential to understand that coin collecting is more than just acquiring coins; it's about building a collection that resonates with your personal interests and values.

The beauty of coin collecting lies in its diversity. Each coin has its own story, reflecting the culture, economy, and history of the time it was minted. Imagine holding a coin that once exchanged hands in a bustling marketplace centuries ago or a rare piece that commemorates a pivotal moment in history. This connection to the past is what makes numismatics so captivating. Whether you're drawn to ancient coins, modern commemoratives, or the thrill of hunting for rare varieties, there's a niche for everyone in this vast world.

As you begin to explore, you may find yourself captivated by the idea of creating a collection that not only showcases your interests but also holds significant value. This is where the practical aspects of coin collecting come into play. Understanding the fundamentals of grading, authentication, and market trends is crucial. It's not just about the coins themselves but also about ensuring that your collection is authentic and valuable. Learning to identify counterfeit coins is a skill that will serve you well, protecting both your investment and your reputation as a collector.

In this journey, you will also encounter the vibrant community of coin collectors. Engaging with fellow enthusiasts—whether online or at local shows—can enhance your experience. Sharing insights, trading stories, and seeking advice from seasoned collectors can provide invaluable knowledge that enriches your understanding of the hobby. Remember, you are not alone in this endeavor; there are countless others who share your passion and are eager to connect.

As you delve deeper into the world of numismatics, consider the legacy you wish to create. Many collectors find joy in the idea of passing down their collections to future generations. This desire to share knowledge and experiences with family can transform your hobby into a meaningful tradition. Imagine sitting down with your children or grandchildren, recounting the tales behind each coin, instilling in them a sense of history and appreciation for the art of collecting. This emotional connection is what elevates coin collecting from a mere hobby to a cherished family legacy.

Additionally, as you navigate the landscape of coin collecting, it's essential to remain vigilant against scams and unscrupulous dealers. The fear of being taken advantage of is a common concern among collectors, especially those who are just starting. To protect yourself, seek out reputable dealers, and consider joining established coin collecting organizations. These resources can provide guidance, offer educational opportunities, and help you build a network of trusted contacts.

Incorporating technology into your collecting journey can also enhance your experience. With the rise of online marketplaces and forums, you have access to a wealth of information at your fingertips. Utilize these platforms to conduct research, compare prices, and engage with other collectors. However, always exercise caution—verify the credibility of sources and be wary of deals that seem too good to be true.

As you embark on this adventure, remember that coin collecting is a personal journey. There is no right or wrong way to build your collection; what matters is that it reflects your interests and passions. Take your time to explore, learn, and enjoy the process. Each coin you acquire will add to your story, creating a tapestry of history that is uniquely yours.

Ultimately, the goal of this book is to equip you with the knowledge and confidence to navigate the world of coin collecting successfully. From understanding the fundamentals to developing a discerning eye for authenticity, we will cover all the essential aspects that will empower you on this journey. So, let's dive in and begin exploring the fascinating world of numismatics together, one coin at a time.

1. Welcome to the World of Coin Collecting

Welcome to the fascinating realm of coin collecting, a journey that transcends mere hobby and transforms into a lifelong passion. As you embark on this adventure, you'll discover that each coin holds a story—stories of empires, economies, and everyday lives. Whether you're drawn to the gleam of precious metals, the thrill of hunting for rare finds, or the desire to connect with history, coin collecting offers a unique blend of excitement and education.

Imagine holding a piece of history in your palm—a coin minted centuries ago, perhaps during the reign of a long-forgotten king. The weight of it, the intricate designs, and even the subtle imperfections tell tales of the past. Each scratch and mark signifies its journey through time, from one hand to another, across continents and cultures. This connection to history is one of the most compelling reasons to collect coins; it allows you to step into the shoes of those who came before us.

As you delve deeper into this world, you'll encounter a diverse community of collectors, each with their own motivations and stories. Some are driven by investment potential, viewing their collections as assets that can appreciate over time. Others are passionate about the artistry of coins, appreciating the craftsmanship that goes into each piece. Then there are those who collect for the thrill of the hunt, spending weekends scouring flea markets and coin shows for that elusive gem. Regardless of your motivation, you'll find camaraderie among fellow collectors, who are often more than willing to share their knowledge and experiences.

However, as with any pursuit, challenges await. The fear of counterfeit coins looms large, especially for those new to the hobby. It's a valid concern, as the market has its fair share of unscrupulous sellers. But fear not; this book is designed to equip you with the tools and knowledge needed to navigate these waters confidently. You'll learn how to authenticate coins, recognize common fakes, and understand the importance of reputable dealers. This knowledge not only protects your investment but also enhances your enjoyment of collecting.

Another critical aspect of coin collecting is the investment potential. Many collectors view their collections as a way to diversify their portfolios. Coins, especially rare or historically significant ones, can appreciate in value over time. However, it's essential to approach this aspect with a clear understanding of the market. We'll delve into investment strategies, helping you to make informed decisions that align with your financial goals. Remember, while collecting can be a lucrative endeavor, it should primarily be about passion and enjoyment.

As you build your collection, consider the legacy you wish to leave behind. Many collectors dream of passing their treasures down to their children, sharing the stories and knowledge that accompany each coin. This aspect of collecting can create lasting family bonds, as you engage your loved ones in the history and significance of your collection. Imagine sitting around the dinner table, recounting tales of the coins you've found and the adventures you've had. It's a wonderful way to involve your family and create memories that will last a lifetime.

Moreover, the world of coin collecting is not limited to your local area. While North American coins may dominate your initial focus, there's a vast array of international coins waiting to be discovered. Exploring the global landscape of numismatics can open new avenues for your collection and provide a broader perspective on the art and history of coinage. You'll find that different cultures have unique stories to tell through their coins, enriching your understanding of the world.

As you embark on this journey, remember that coin collecting is not just about acquiring pieces; it's about the stories they tell and the connections you make along the way. Whether you're attending local coin shows, participating in online forums, or simply sharing your passion with friends and family, each interaction adds depth to your collecting experience.

In conclusion, welcome to the world of coin collecting, where history, art, and investment converge. Embrace the journey ahead, armed with the knowledge and passion that will guide you through the intricacies of this rewarding hobby. With each coin you add to your collection, you're not just accumulating wealth; you're building a bridge to the past and creating a legacy for the fut

The Fascination of Numismatics

Numismatics is more than just a hobby; it is a profound journey through history, culture, and human achievement. Imagine holding a coin in your hand that has traveled through time, witnessing significant events and embodying the stories of those who once possessed it. Each coin serves as a tangible link to the past, a piece of art that reflects the values and aspirations of the society that minted it. The fascination of numismatics lies in its ability to transcend mere monetary value, inviting collectors to explore the rich tapestry of human experience.

As you delve into the world of coin collecting, you may find yourself captivated by the intricate designs that adorn each piece. From the majestic portraits of emperors and leaders to the symbols of national pride, every detail tells a story. Consider the iconic American Silver Eagle, a coin that not only represents the strength of the nation but also embodies the ideals of freedom and resilience. As you admire its beauty, you can't help but wonder about the hands that have held it before you, the transactions it has facilitated, and the historical moments it has witnessed.

For many collectors, the thrill of the hunt is a significant part of the allure. The search for that elusive coin, the one that completes a collection or fills a gap in your knowledge, ignites a sense of adventure. Picture yourself at a bustling coin show, surrounded by fellow enthusiasts, each with their own stories and treasures. The air is filled with excitement as you sift through trays of coins, engaging in conversations that spark your curiosity and deepen your understanding of this fascinating field. In these moments, you realize that numismatics is not just about the coins; it's about the connections you forge with others who share your passion.

However, the journey is not without its challenges. The world of numismatics can be daunting, especially for newcomers. The fear of acquiring counterfeit coins looms large, casting a shadow over the joy of collecting. This concern is valid and should not be taken lightly. As you navigate this intricate landscape, it's essential to equip yourself with the knowledge and tools necessary to protect your investment and reputation. Understanding the signs of authenticity and knowing where to seek professional advice can empower you to make informed decisions, transforming anxiety into confidence.

Moreover, the emotional aspect of collecting should not be underestimated. Many collectors find solace in their coins, using them as a means to connect with their family and pass down stories from generation to generation. Imagine sitting around the dinner table, sharing the history behind a rare coin with your children, instilling in them a sense of wonder and appreciation for the past. This legacy transcends the physical coins themselves; it is about imparting values, fostering curiosity, and creating lasting memories.

As you embark on this numismatic journey, allow yourself to be open to the myriad of experiences that await you. Embrace the thrill of discovery, the camaraderie of fellow collectors, and the joy of building a collection that holds personal significance. Each coin you acquire is not just a piece of metal; it is a chapter in your own story, a reflection of your interests, and a legacy you can share with those you love. In this way, numismatics becomes not just a hobby, but a meaningful pursuit that enriches your life and the lives of those around you.

Ultimately, the fascination of numismatics lies in its ability to connect us with the past while simultaneously shaping our future. As you explore this captivating world, remember that each coin you collect is an invitation to delve deeper into history, to engage with others, and to create a legacy that will endure for generations. The journey is as important as the destination, and with each step you take, you will uncover not only the beauty of coins but also the profound stories they tell.

Why Collect Coins?

Collecting coins is more than just a hobby; it's a journey into history, art, and personal connection. Each coin tells a story, a fragment of time captured in metal. As you hold a coin in your hand, you're not just examining its surface; you're engaging with the past, exploring the civilizations that created it, and understanding the economies that flourished or faltered. This intrinsic value is what draws many into the world of numismatics.

For many collectors, the thrill of the hunt is a significant part of the experience. Imagine walking through a bustling coin show, the excitement palpable in the air. Vendors proudly display their wares, each coin a unique treasure waiting to be discovered. It's a community of enthusiasts, where stories are exchanged, and friendships are forged. The shared passion for collecting creates bonds that often last a lifetime. Whether you're a beginner or a seasoned collector, the camaraderie found in this community is invaluable.

But beyond the social aspects, coin collecting offers a sense of accomplishment. There is something deeply satisfying about carefully curating a collection, each piece representing a milestone in your journey. Perhaps you started with a few coins from your childhood, and over the years, your collection has evolved into a diverse assortment of rare finds. Each addition is a testament to your dedication and knowledge, a reflection of your personal taste and interests. This journey can also serve as a meaningful legacy, something to pass down to your children, allowing them to share in the joy and history of your collection.

As you delve deeper into the world of coins, you'll discover that collecting can also be a wise financial investment. While the market can fluctuate, certain coins appreciate in value over time, making them not just collectibles but potential assets. However, this aspect of collecting requires a careful approach. Understanding market trends, recognizing which coins hold their value, and learning how to authenticate them are crucial skills for any serious collector. This knowledge not only protects your investment but also enhances your enjoyment of the hobby. You'll find that the more you learn, the more confident you become in your decisions.

Yet, it's essential to approach coin collecting with a critical eye. The fear of counterfeits is a valid concern for many collectors. As you navigate through local shows or online marketplaces, the potential for deception lurks in the shadows. This is where your diligence pays off. Educating yourself on authentication techniques and seeking guidance from reputable sources can help you avoid pitfalls. Building a network of trusted dealers and fellow collectors can also provide a safety net, ensuring that you're making informed purchases.

Moreover, the emotional connection to your collection can be profound. Each coin can evoke memories, whether it's a piece you found during a family trip or one that was gifted to you by a loved one. These stories add layers of meaning to your collection, transforming it from a mere assortment of metal into a tapestry of personal history. As you share these stories with your children, you're not just passing down coins; you're imparting lessons about history, value, and the importance of pursuing one's passions.

In this way, coin collecting transcends the act of accumulation. It becomes a way to engage with history, connect with others, and create a legacy. The journey is as important as the destination, and every coin is a milestone along the way. As you embark on your collecting adventure, embrace the stories, the friendships, and the knowledge you'll gain. Each coin is an opportunity to explore the past, enrich your present, and inspire the future.

In conclusion, the reasons to collect coins are as varied as the coins themselves. Whether you're drawn in by the history, the thrill of the hunt, the potential for investment, or the desire to create a lasting legacy, there's no denying that coin collecting is a fulfilling pursuit. As you build your collection, remember to enjoy the journey, seek out knowledge, and share your passion with others. After all, it's not just about the coins; it's about the stories they tell and the connections they foster.

How to Use This Book

Welcome to your journey into the world of coin collecting. This book is designed not just as a guide, but as a companion for your exploration of numismatics. Whether you're a novice just starting to uncover the beauty and history behind each coin or an experienced collector looking to deepen your knowledge, you'll find valuable insights that resonate with your passion. As you turn these pages, envision yourself in a conversation with a seasoned collector who is eager to share their experiences, tips, and stories.

In the vast realm of coin collecting, it's easy to feel overwhelmed by the sheer volume of information available. That's why this book is structured to flow naturally, guiding you through the essential aspects of building and maintaining a collection. You'll discover practical advice woven into engaging narratives, making complex concepts more accessible. With each chapter, you'll find yourself not just learning, but also reflecting on your own collecting journey.

As you dive into the chapters, keep in mind that each section is crafted to stand on its own. You won't encounter repetitive content, as each topic is approached with a fresh perspective. This ensures that your reading experience remains engaging and informative, allowing you to absorb knowledge without feeling like you're revisiting familiar territory. Each chapter will build upon your understanding without overshadowing the unique insights offered in the others.

Throughout this book, you'll encounter stories that highlight the emotional connections collectors forge with their coins. These anecdotes serve to remind you that coin collecting is not merely a hobby; it's a way to create a legacy, a bridge to the past that can be shared with future generations. You'll find yourself inspired by tales of collectors who have turned their passion into a family tradition, emphasizing the importance of involving loved ones in this rewarding pursuit.

Furthermore, you'll learn about the critical aspects of authenticity and investment strategies. This is particularly important for those of you who approach collecting with a meticulous mindset, much like you would in your professional life. You'll gain insights into identifying counterfeits and understanding the value of your collection, equipping you with the knowledge needed to navigate this intricate landscape with confidence.

As you progress through the book, take a moment to reflect on your own experiences and aspirations as a collector. What drives your passion? What stories do you wish to pass down to your children? This book encourages you to engage with these questions, as they are integral to your journey in numismatics.

In addition to the narratives and insights, you'll find interactive elements designed to enhance your reading experience. These features will allow you to self-assess your knowledge and reflect on what you've learned. Consider keeping a journal alongside this book, where you can jot down your thoughts, questions, and discoveries. This practice not only reinforces your learning but also creates a personal record of your collecting journey.

Ultimately, this book is more than just a resource; it's an invitation to immerse yourself in the fascinating world of coins. As you read, let the stories and advice resonate with your own experiences.

Embrace the challenges and triumphs that come with collecting, and remember that you are part of a vibrant community of enthusiasts who share your passion. Together, we can celebrate the rich history and artistry behind each coin, fostering connections that transcend time and generations.

So, as you embark on this adventure, keep an open mind and a curious heart. The world of coin collecting awaits you, filled with treasures and tales just waiting to be discovered.

Book 2: The Basics of Coinage

As you delve into the world of coinage, it's essential to understand that coins are not just pieces of metal; they are tangible pieces of history. Each coin tells a story, reflecting the culture, economy, and artistry of the time it was minted. Imagine holding a coin that once passed through the hands of a Roman emperor or a revolutionary figure. The excitement of connecting with the past is what draws many collectors into this fascinating hobby.

Every coin has its own unique characteristics, including its **denomination**, **composition**, and **design**. These elements come together to create a coin's identity. For instance, consider the American penny. Originally minted in 1792, it has undergone various changes in design and composition over the years. The transition from the copper penny to the zinc-coated version we see today illustrates how economic factors influence coinage. Understanding these changes helps collectors appreciate the historical context behind each coin they acquire.

When you start collecting, it's important to familiarize yourself with the different **types of coins** available. From ancient coins to modern commemoratives, each type offers a unique glimpse into its era. Ancient coins, often made of precious metals, can be particularly alluring due to their rarity and the stories they carry. On the other hand, modern coins, such as state quarters or presidential dollars, provide a more accessible entry point for new collectors. Each type has its own appeal, and the journey of discovering what resonates with you is part of the joy of collecting.

As you explore the world of coinage, you'll encounter various **grading systems** that help determine a coin's condition and value. Grading is an art in itself, requiring careful observation and practice. Coins are typically graded on a scale from one to seventy, with one being heavily worn and seventy representing a perfect specimen. Learning how to grade coins not only enhances your collecting experience but also empowers you to make informed decisions when buying or selling. Imagine confidently identifying a rare coin in mint condition, knowing its potential value and historical significance.

One of the most exhilarating aspects of coin collecting is the thrill of the hunt. Whether you're scouring local coin shops, attending auctions, or exploring online marketplaces, each search can yield unexpected treasures. It's essential to approach these opportunities with a discerning eye, especially when it comes to **authenticity**. Counterfeit coins are unfortunately prevalent, and knowing how to spot them is crucial. Look for inconsistencies in weight, design, and finish. Additionally, consider investing in tools like a digital scale or a magnifying glass to aid in your assessments. The peace of mind that comes from knowing you've made an authentic purchase is invaluable.

Engaging with the community can significantly enhance your collecting journey. Coin shows and local clubs offer not only a chance to buy and sell but also to connect with fellow enthusiasts. Sharing stories, tips, and experiences enriches your understanding and appreciation of the hobby. You might find a mentor who can guide you through the intricacies of coin collecting or even forge lifelong friendships. The sense of camaraderie among collectors is one of the most rewarding aspects of this pursuit.

As you build your collection, consider the **legacy** you wish to create. Many collectors are motivated by the desire to pass down their passion and knowledge to future generations. Involving your family in your collecting journey can be a fulfilling experience. Perhaps you could start a family tradition of visiting coin shows together or even create a shared collection that tells your family's story. This not only strengthens family bonds but also instills a sense of history and appreciation for the art of numismatics.

In conclusion, the basics of coinage extend far beyond the coins themselves. They encompass history, artistry, and personal connection. As you embark on your collecting journey, remember that each coin is a portal to the past, waiting to be explored. Embrace the excitement of discovery, the thrill of the hunt, and the joy of sharing your passion with others. With each coin you acquire, you're not just building a collection; you're creating a legacy that can be cherished for generations to come.

2. History of Coinage

The earliest known coins date back to the first millennium B.C.Coined in Lydia(present-day Turkey) dolly in gold or electro(gold+silver),they bore the royal seal to guarantee their value

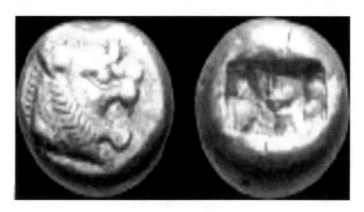

The first coins

The history of coinage is a fascinating journey that spans thousands of years, reflecting the evolution of societies, economies, and cultures. At its core, coinage began as a practical solution to the challenges of trade. Before coins, bartering was the norm, which often led to complications in transactions. The invention of coinage simplified trade by providing a standardized medium of exchange. The first coins are believed to have been minted in the ancient kingdom of Lydia around 600 BCE, made from a naturally occurring alloy of gold and silver known as electrum.

As coinage spread, it became a symbol of power and authority. Rulers used coins not only for economic transactions but also as a means of propaganda. Coins often featured the likeness of the monarch, along with inscriptions that conveyed messages of legitimacy and strength. This practice established a direct connection between the ruler and the people, reinforcing the idea that the coin was a representation of the state itself.

The design and material of coins evolved over time. In ancient Greece, coins were made from silver and featured intricate designs that showcased local deities or significant events. The Romans took this further, standardizing coinage across their vast empire, which facilitated trade and commerce on an unprecedented scale. The Roman denarius became a benchmark for currency, influencing coinage in various cultures long after the fall of the empire.

During the Middle Ages, the introduction of gold and silver coins marked a significant shift in the economy. The use of precious metals not only increased the value of coins but also led to the rise of minting as a regulated practice. Various kingdoms minted their own coins, which often led to confusion and disputes over value. This period saw the emergence of coinage as an essential tool for establishing trade routes and economic stability.

As the Renaissance dawned, coinage experienced another transformation. The introduction of new technologies, such as the screw press, allowed for more precise minting processes, leading to coins with sharper details and more intricate designs. This era also saw the rise of banknotes, which began to replace coins as a more convenient means of conducting large transactions. However, coins remained a vital part of daily commerce, especially for smaller purchases.

In modern times, the role of coinage has continued to evolve. The establishment of central banks and the introduction of fiat currency shifted the focus from coins as a representation of tangible value to their role as a tool for economic policy. Today, coins are produced in various denominations, often featuring national symbols and historical figures, serving as a reminder of a nation's heritage and values.

Despite the rise of digital currency and electronic payments, coins still hold a significant place in the hearts of collectors and historians alike. The allure of coin collecting lies not just in the monetary value but in the stories each coin tells—stories of trade, power, culture, and history. As collectors delve into the world of numismatics, they engage with a rich tapestry that connects them to the past, allowing them to appreciate the artistry and significance of coinage throughout the ages.

Understanding the history of coinage is crucial for any collector. It provides context for the coins they seek and helps them appreciate the nuances of minting practices, regional variations, and historical significance. This knowledge not only enhances the collecting experience but also equips collectors with the tools to make informed decisions in their pursuit of building a meaningful collection.

The evolution of **coinage** is a fascinating journey that reflects the economic, social, and technological changes throughout history. It all began with the need for a reliable medium of exchange. Before coins, trade was conducted through barter, which often proved inefficient. The introduction of coins revolutionized this system, providing a standardized unit of value that could be easily recognized and traded.

The first coins are believed to have been minted in **Lydia** (modern-day Turkey) around 600 BCE. These early coins were made from electrum, a naturally occurring alloy of gold and silver, and featured simple designs that indicated their authenticity and value. The transition from barter to coinage was not just a practical advancement; it also marked a significant cultural shift, as coins began to bear the images of rulers and deities, serving as a form of propaganda and a means to establish authority.

As trade routes expanded, so did the use of coins. The **Greeks** and later the **Romans** adopted and adapted the concept, creating coins that varied in size, weight, and material. Roman coins, in particular, became a powerful tool for the empire, facilitating trade across vast territories and helping to unify diverse cultures under a common currency. The designs on Roman coins often celebrated military victories, significant events, or notable figures, further embedding the coins into the social fabric of the time.

With the fall of the Roman Empire, Europe entered a period known as the **Dark Ages**, during which coinage became less standardized. Local currencies emerged, often reflecting the feudal systems in place. However, the **Middle Ages** saw a resurgence in coinage, driven by the growth of trade and commerce. The introduction of **minting techniques** improved the quality and security of coins, reducing the prevalence of counterfeiting.

The **Renaissance** brought about significant advancements in art and technology, which were reflected in the design of coins. This period saw the introduction of intricate designs and the use of new materials, including copper and bronze, alongside gold and silver. The artistic value of coins began to be appreciated, leading to the rise of collectors who sought out unique pieces.

As nations began to form and assert their identities, coinage became a symbol of national pride. The **Industrial Revolution** further transformed coin production, introducing machinery that allowed for mass production and standardization. This made coins more accessible to the general public and facilitated international trade.

In the 20th century, the introduction of **paper currency** and digital transactions began to challenge the dominance of coins. However, coins have persisted, adapting to modern needs. Commemorative coins, for instance, have emerged as a way to celebrate significant events or figures, appealing to collectors and investors alike.

Today, the world of coinage is more diverse than ever. Collectors can explore a vast array of coins from different eras and regions, each telling its own story. The rise of the internet has also transformed the way collectors buy, sell, and trade coins, making it easier to connect with others who share their passion.Understanding the history of coinage is essential for any collector. It provides context for the coins they seek and helps them appreciate the artistry and significance behind each piece. As collectors delve into the past, they not only build their collections but also contribute to the preservation of history, ensuring that the stories behind these remarkable artifacts are not forgotten.

In summary, the journey of coinage is a testament to human innovation and resilience. From its humble beginnings in ancient Lydia to the complexities of modern numismatics, coins have played a crucial role in shaping economies and cultures throughout history. For collectors, this rich tapestry of history offers endless opportunities for exploration and discovery.

The Evolution of Money

The concept of money has undergone a profound transformation throughout history, evolving from simple barter systems to complex digital currencies. Understanding this evolution is crucial for any coin collector, as it provides context for the coins they collect and the value those coins hold.

Initially, people relied on **barter**, exchanging goods and services directly without a standardized medium. This system had its limitations, primarily due to the difficulty in finding mutual needs. For instance, a farmer with grain might struggle to find a blacksmith who needed grain at the same time. This inefficiency led to the need for a more practical solution.

As societies advanced, various forms of **money** emerged, including commodity money, which included items like salt, cattle, or grain—things inherently valuable in their own right. Eventually, metals became the preferred medium due to their durability and divisibility. The introduction of **precious metals** like gold and silver marked a significant milestone in the evolution of money, as these metals were widely accepted and recognized for their value.

The first coins were minted in the ancient kingdom of Lydia around 600 BCE, made from electrum, a natural alloy of gold and silver. These coins standardized value and simplified trade, paving the way for more complex economic systems. The use of coins spread quickly across cultures, with different regions minting their own versions, often stamped with symbols or images that represented their rulers or deities.

As empires expanded, so did the use of **currency**. The Roman Empire, for instance, introduced a sophisticated monetary system that included various denominations of coins, facilitating trade across vast territories. The Roman denarius became a standard currency, widely used and trusted, which helped unify the economy across different regions.

However, as economies grew, the limitations of physical coins became apparent. Carrying large amounts of metal was impractical for many transactions. This led to the development of **paper money**, which first appeared in China during the Tang Dynasty (618–907 CE). By the Song Dynasty (960–1279 CE), paper currency had gained widespread acceptance, making transactions more convenient and efficient.

In Europe, the introduction of banknotes occurred much later, around the 17th century, when banks began issuing promissory notes that could be exchanged for coins. This innovation laid the groundwork for modern banking systems and the concept of **fiat currency**, which is money that has value not because of its intrinsic properties but because a government maintains it and people have faith in its value.

As we moved into the 20th century, the world saw the emergence of **digital currency** and electronic transactions, revolutionizing how we think about money. The advent of credit cards and online banking changed the landscape, allowing for instantaneous transactions without the need for physical currency. Today, we are witnessing the rise of cryptocurrencies, such as Bitcoin, which operate on decentralized networks using blockchain technology. This new form of money challenges traditional financial systems and raises questions about the future of currency.

For coin collectors, understanding the evolution of money is essential. It not only helps contextualize the coins they collect but also informs their investment strategies. Recognizing how historical events influenced the value of coins can aid collectors in making informed decisions about their collections. Moreover, as new forms of currency emerge, collectors must stay abreast of trends to avoid potential pitfalls and scams in the market.

In conclusion, the evolution of money is a fascinating journey that reflects the changing needs and values of society. From barter to digital currencies, each phase has contributed to our understanding of wealth and exchange. As collectors dive into the world of numismatics, they will find that this history enriches their experience, allowing them to appreciate not just the coins themselves but the stories and economies behind them.

From barter to currency: Around 296 B.C. coinage began to be produced, an abstract form of payment, initially made from precious metals:gold, silver and copper

Significant Historica Coins

Throughout history, certain coins have transcended their monetary value to become symbols of cultural significance and historical importance. Collecting these coins not only provides a glimpse into the past but also offers a unique opportunity to own a piece of history. Here are some of the most significant historical coins that every collector should consider.

Ancient Coins

Ancient coins, such as those from the **Greek** and **Roman** empires, are among the most sought-after collectibles. These coins often feature intricate designs and are made from precious metals like gold and silver. The **Greek drachma** and the **Roman denarius** are prime examples, each telling stories of trade, politics, and daily life in ancient civilizations. Collectors appreciate the rarity and historical context of these coins, making them a valuable addition to any collection.

Medieval Coins

During the medieval period, coins began to reflect the power and influence of monarchies. The **English penny** and the **French livre** are notable examples, often featuring the likeness of kings and queens. These coins not only served as currency but also as propaganda tools, celebrating the reign and accomplishments of rulers. Collecting medieval coins can provide insights into the socio-political climate of the time, making them fascinating artifacts for history enthusiasts.

Colonial Coins

As exploration and colonization spread, so did the minting of coins in various regions. Coins like the **Spanish real** became widely circulated in the Americas, influencing local economies. The

Massachusetts Bay Colony pine tree shilling is another rare find, representing early American history and the struggle for independence. Collectors often seek these coins for their historical significance and the stories they tell about early trade and commerce.

Commemorative Coins

Commemorative coins are minted to honor significant events, people, or anniversaries. For example, the **U.S. Bicentennial coin** celebrated the 200th anniversary of American independence, while coins featuring **Martin Luther King Jr.** commemorate his impact on civil rights. These coins often have limited mintage, increasing their desirability among collectors. They serve as reminders of pivotal moments in history and can spark meaningful conversations about the events they commemorate.

Modern Coins

Modern coins, minted in the last century, can also hold significant historical value. The **American Eagle** and **Canadian Maple Leaf** are popular among collectors, not just for their aesthetic appeal but also for their precious metal content. Additionally, coins that mark important anniversaries, such as the **50th anniversary of the moon landing**, can become highly sought after. Collectors often appreciate the blend of artistry and history found in these coins.

Investment Potential

Investing in significant historical coins can be both rewarding and financially beneficial. Coins with historical importance often appreciate in value over time, making them a viable investment option. However, it's crucial to conduct thorough research and ensure authenticity before making any purchases. Engaging with reputable dealers and attending coin shows can provide opportunities to acquire these valuable pieces while also expanding your knowledge.

Preserving Your Collection

Once you've acquired significant historical coins, proper preservation is essential. Store coins in **acid-free holders** or **coin capsules** to protect them from environmental damage. Avoid cleaning coins, as this can diminish their value. Regularly inspect your collection for signs of deterioration and consider investing in a safe or a bank safety deposit box for high-value items. By taking these steps, you can ensure that your historical coins remain in excellent condition for years to come.

Building a Legacy

Collecting significant historical coins is more than just a hobby; it's an opportunity to create a legacy. As you build your collection, consider sharing your passion with family and friends. Educate your children about the history behind each coin and the importance of preserving these artifacts. By involving your loved ones, you not only enrich their understanding of history but also foster a sense of connection and appreciation for the past.

The Impact of Coins on Society and Culture

Coins have always played a significant role in shaping societies and cultures throughout history. From their inception, they have served not merely as a medium of exchange but also as symbols of power, artistry, and identity. The designs on coins often reflect the values, beliefs, and historical events of the time, providing a tangible connection to the past. **Understanding the cultural impact of coins enriches our appreciation for numismatics** and highlights the stories behind each piece.

One of the most fascinating aspects of coins is their ability to act as a reflection of a society's values. For instance, ancient Roman coins often depicted emperors and gods, illustrating the importance of leadership and divinity in Roman culture. This practice was not just about currency; it was a way of reinforcing the legitimacy and divine right of rulers. **Coins became tools of propaganda**, spreading messages of power and authority across the vast Roman Empire.

Similarly, coins have been used to commemorate significant events or figures. The introduction of commemorative coins in various cultures serves as a means to celebrate national pride, historical milestones, or influential leaders. For example, the U.S. Mint has issued numerous commemorative coins to honor everything from the 50th anniversary of statehood to notable figures in American history. **These coins serve as reminders of collective memory**, encapsulating important moments that resonate with citizens.

Coins also offer a glimpse into the economic conditions of their time. The composition, size, and weight of coins can indicate the wealth and resources available to a society. For example, during times of prosperity, coins might be minted from precious metals, while during economic downturns, governments may resort to debasing currency by using less valuable materials. **This shift in coinage reflects broader economic trends** and can be a valuable tool for historians studying the rise and fall of civilizations.

Furthermore, the artistic designs on coins reveal much about the cultural aesthetics of a period. The intricate details and craftsmanship of coin designs can reflect the artistic movements of their time, showcasing the skills of engravers and artists. For example, the stunning designs of Renaissance coins often featured elaborate portraits and intricate motifs, highlighting the era's emphasis on art and beauty. **Coins become miniature canvases**, preserving the artistic heritage of a culture for future generations.

Coins also serve as a means of social cohesion. In many cultures, the act of coin collecting has fostered communities and relationships among collectors. Local coin clubs and online forums provide spaces for enthusiasts to share their knowledge, trade coins, and discuss their passion. **This sense of community** can be particularly appealing to those who may feel isolated in their collecting endeavors, as it creates opportunities for social interaction and learning.

The legacy of coins extends beyond their immediate use in transactions; they often become heirlooms passed down through generations. Families may share stories about the coins they collect, instilling a sense of history and belonging in younger members. This aspect of coin collecting can be especially meaningful for collectors who wish to create a lasting legacy for their children. **Coins thus become vessels of family history**, connecting generations through shared interests and stories.

In addition to their cultural significance, coins can also serve as a form of investment. Many collectors view coins not only as items of beauty but also as assets that can appreciate over time. This dual purpose of coins—as both collectibles and investments—has led to a thriving market where individuals can buy, sell, and trade based on their value. **Understanding the market dynamics** and the historical significance of certain coins can empower collectors to make informed decisions about their investments.

However, with the rise of the internet and online marketplaces, the potential for scams and counterfeit coins has increased. Collectors must be vigilant and educated about authentication techniques to protect their investments and reputations. Knowledge about the historical context and the specific features of coins can help collectors avoid pitfalls and ensure they are acquiring genuine pieces. **This aspect of numismatics emphasizes the importance of education** and community engagement in the collecting process.

In conclusion, coins are much more than mere currency; they are cultural artifacts that encapsulate the values, history, and artistry of the societies that produced them. The impact of coins on society and culture is profound, influencing everything from economic practices to social relationships. For collectors, understanding this impact enhances their appreciation for the hobby and underscores the significance of each piece within a broader historical narrative. **As you embark on your numismatic journey**, remember that every coin tells a story, and in each collection lies the potential to connect with the past while shaping the future.

3. Understanding Numismatics

Numismatics is more than just the study of coins; it's a fascinating journey through history, culture, and economics. Collectors often find themselves captivated by the stories that each coin tells, reflecting the society and era from which it originated. Understanding numismatics requires an appreciation for the intricate details that make each piece unique, as well as a grasp of the broader context in which these coins were minted.

At its core, **numismatics** encompasses the collection and study of currency, including coins, tokens, paper money, and medals. It serves as a bridge connecting collectors to the past, allowing them to explore the evolution of currency and its role in human civilization. From ancient Roman denarii to modern-day bullion coins, each item in a collection can provide insights into the economic conditions, political climates, and artistic trends of its time.

One of the most rewarding aspects of numismatics is the opportunity to engage with a community of like-minded individuals. Many collectors find joy in sharing their passion with others, whether through local coin clubs, online forums, or national conventions. These interactions not only foster friendships but also provide valuable resources for learning and growth. As you delve deeper into the world of coins, you'll discover that the relationships you build can enhance your collecting experience significantly.

Another critical element of understanding numismatics is recognizing the **importance of authentication**. In a field where counterfeits can easily deceive even seasoned collectors, having a solid grasp of how to identify genuine coins is paramount. This involves learning about various minting techniques, understanding the characteristics of specific coins, and utilizing modern technology for verification. As you hone these skills, you'll gain confidence in your ability to discern the real from the fake, ensuring that your collection remains a source of pride rather than concern.

Moreover, the investment aspect of numismatics cannot be overlooked. Many collectors view their hobby as a way to build wealth over time, and understanding market trends, grading systems, and valuation methods is essential. While some coins can appreciate significantly in value, others may not hold the same potential. Educating yourself about the factors that influence coin values, such as rarity, demand, and condition, will empower you to make informed purchasing decisions that align with your collecting goals.

The emotional connection that many collectors have with their coins is another facet of numismatics worth exploring. Coins often carry personal significance, whether they are heirlooms passed down through generations or pieces acquired during memorable travels. This emotional investment can deepen your appreciation for the hobby and motivate you to share it with your family. Involving your children in the collecting process can create lasting memories and instill a sense of history and value that transcends the monetary worth of the coins themselves.

As you navigate the world of numismatics, remember that this journey is as much about personal growth and discovery as it is about the coins themselves. Embrace the learning process, seek out knowledge, and connect with others who share your passion. The more you understand the complexities of numismatics, the richer your collecting experience will become.

Key Terms and Concepts

The world of coin collecting is rich with **terminology** that can seem daunting at first. Understanding these key terms is essential for any collector, whether you're just starting out or looking to deepen your knowledge. Here are some fundamental concepts that will help you navigate the fascinating realm of numismatics.

Numismatics

Numismatics is the study or collection of currency, including coins, tokens, paper money, and related objects. It encompasses not just the collecting aspect, but also the historical, cultural, and artistic significance of currency throughout time. As a collector, embracing this broader perspective can enhance your appreciation of your collection.

Grade

The term **grade** refers to the condition of a coin, which is crucial for determining its value. Coins are graded on a scale that ranges from **Poor** (P) to **Mint State** (MS), with various intermediate grades such as **Fine** (F) and **Very Fine** (VF). Understanding grading helps collectors make informed decisions about purchases and sales.

Authentication

Authentication is the process of verifying the genuineness of a coin. This is vital in avoiding counterfeits, which can be prevalent in the market. Techniques for authentication can include examining **mint marks**, **weight**, and **metal composition**, as well as using advanced technology like **X-ray fluorescence** (XRF) analysis.

Mint Mark

A **mint mark** is a letter or symbol stamped on a coin that indicates where it was produced. Different mints can produce variations of the same coin, which can affect its rarity and value. Familiarizing yourself with mint marks is essential for understanding the nuances of your collection.

Proof Coin

A **proof coin** is specially made for collectors, featuring a higher quality strike and a polished finish. These coins are typically produced in limited quantities and can be significantly more valuable than their regular counterparts. Knowing the difference between proof and circulation coins can help you make strategic decisions in your collecting journey.

Variety

Variety refers to a specific type of coin that has distinct characteristics differing from the standard issue. This can include differences in design, minting errors, or alterations made during production. Collectors often seek out varieties as they can be more valuable and sought after than standard coins.

Counterfeit

A **counterfeit** coin is a fake coin made with the intent to deceive collectors or investors. Recognizing counterfeits is crucial, as they can diminish the value of your collection and tarnish your reputation. Learning to identify common counterfeiting techniques is an essential skill for any serious collector.

Market Value

Market value refers to the price a coin can realistically fetch in the current market. This value can fluctuate based on demand, rarity, and condition. Staying informed about market trends and values can help you make wise investment choices.

Historical Significance

The **historical significance** of a coin can greatly enhance its value. Coins that commemorate important events, figures, or periods can be particularly desirable. Understanding the history behind your coins can enrich your collecting experience and provide a story to share with future generations.

Collection

A **collection** refers to a group of coins that a collector has assembled. Collections can vary widely in focus, from specific types of coins, like **silver dollars**, to thematic collections based on historical events or geographical regions. Defining the focus of your collection can help guide your purchasing decisions.

Investment

Investment in coins involves purchasing coins with the expectation that their value will increase over time. This can be a rewarding venture, but it requires careful consideration of market trends, rarity, and the overall condition of the coins. A well-informed collector can build a collection that not only provides enjoyment but also financial returns.

Condition

The **condition** of a coin is a critical factor in its value. Coins are assessed based on their wear and tear, which can be influenced by factors such as handling, storage, and environmental exposure. Maintaining the condition of your coins through proper storage and handling techniques is essential for preserving their value.

Set

A **set** is a complete grouping of coins that share a common theme, such as a specific year or type. Many collectors aim to complete sets, which can enhance the overall value and appeal of their collection. Understanding the components of various sets can help you identify gaps in your own collection.

Dealer

A **dealer** is an individual or business that buys and sells coins. Building a relationship with reputable dealers can be beneficial for collectors, as they can provide valuable insights and access to rare coins. It's important to choose dealers who are knowledgeable and trustworthy to ensure fair transactions.

Show

A **show** refers to an event where collectors and dealers gather to buy, sell, and trade coins. Attending shows can provide opportunities for networking, learning, and discovering unique coins. Engaging with the community at shows can also enhance your collecting experience.

Registry

A **registry** is a system that allows collectors to register their coins and compete with others based on the quality and completeness of their collections. Many collectors find this a motivating factor, as it encourages them to improve their collections and connect with like-minded individuals.

Attribution

Attribution is the process of identifying a coin's specific type, variety, or historical significance. Proper attribution is essential for accurately assessing a coin's value and rarity. Many collectors keep detailed records of their coins' attributions to track their collections effectively.

Heritage

Heritage refers to the historical and cultural background associated with a coin. Understanding the heritage of your coins can deepen your appreciation and provide context for their significance. This knowledge can also be valuable when discussing your collection with others.

Rarity

Rarity is a key factor in determining a coin's value. Coins that are produced in limited quantities or have unique features are often more sought after by collectors. Recognizing the rarity of coins in your collection can help you assess their potential investment value.

Condition Census

The **condition census** is a ranking of the highest-quality examples of a specific coin type. It provides collectors with a benchmark for assessing the quality of their own coins. Being aware of the condition census can guide your purchasing decisions and help you understand the competitive landscape of your collection.

Documentation

Documentation includes any records, certificates, or appraisals related to your coins. Keeping thorough documentation is vital for proving authenticity and value, especially if you plan to sell or pass on your collection. It also adds credibility to your collection and can enhance its appeal to potential buyers.

By familiarizing yourself with these essential terms and concepts, you'll be better equipped to navigate the world of coin collecting with confidence. Each term represents a piece of the larger puzzle, helping you build a collection that is not only valuable but also meaningful for you and your family.

The Various Types of Coins

When diving into the world of numismatics, it's essential to understand the **various types of coins** that exist. This knowledge not only enhances your appreciation of coin collecting but also aids in making informed purchasing decisions. Coins can be categorized based on several criteria, including their **material composition**, **design**, and **origin**.

Material Composition

Coins are typically made from a variety of metals, each contributing to their value and collectibility. Common materials include:

- **Gold:** Known for its intrinsic value, gold coins are often sought after for both their beauty and investment potential.

- **Silver:** Silver coins have a long history and are popular among collectors, especially those interested in **silver bullion**.

- **Copper:** Often found in older coins, copper has historical significance and can be a fascinating area of study.

- **Nickel:** Many modern coins incorporate nickel, which is durable and resistant to corrosion.

- **Alloys:** Some coins are made from a combination of metals, such as bronze or cupronickel, which can affect their appearance and value.

Design

The design of a coin plays a crucial role in its appeal and collectibility. Coins can be categorized as:

- **Circulating Coins:** These are the everyday coins you use for transactions. They often feature common designs and are produced in large quantities.

- **Commemorative Coins:** Issued to celebrate a specific event or person, these coins are often produced in limited quantities and can be highly sought after.

- **Proof Coins:** Created for collectors, proof coins are struck multiple times to ensure a high-quality finish and are usually sold at a premium.

- **Varieties and Errors:** Coins can also be classified based on unique characteristics or errors during production, which can significantly increase their value.

Origin

The origin of a coin often influences its value and desirability. Coins can be categorized by:

- **Ancient Coins:** These coins come from ancient civilizations and can be fascinating for their historical significance.

- **Modern Coins:** Typically minted from the 20th century onward, these coins often reflect contemporary themes and designs.

- **International Coins:** Collecting coins from around the world can provide insight into different cultures and histories, making it an enriching experience.

- **Local Coins:** Every country has its own minting practices, and local coins can often tell a story about that region's economic history.

Collectibility Factors

When considering which types of coins to collect, several factors can influence their collectibility:

- **Rarity:** The fewer coins that exist, the more valuable they tend to be. Understanding the mintage numbers can help you gauge rarity.

- **Condition:** The state of a coin, often graded on a scale, can significantly affect its value. Coins in better condition are usually more desirable.

- **Historical Significance:** Coins that have a unique story or are linked to important events can captivate collectors.

- **Market Trends:** Keeping an eye on market trends can help you make informed decisions about which types of coins to invest in.

Understanding the **various types of coins** is a crucial step in building a successful collection. By familiarizing yourself with the different categories based on material, design, and origin, you can make informed choices that align with your collecting goals. This knowledge will not only enhance your collecting experience but also help you avoid potential pitfalls, such as purchasing counterfeit coins or overpaying for common pieces. Remember, the journey of coin collecting is as valuable as the coins themselves, and with each piece you acquire, you're adding to a legacy that can be shared with future generations.

Introduction to Coin Grading

Coin grading is an essential aspect of numismatics that helps collectors understand the value and condition of their coins. The grading process assesses a coin's quality based on various criteria, including its physical characteristics, surface preservation, and overall appearance. Understanding these factors is crucial for anyone looking to build a significant collection or make informed purchasing decisions.

The **grade** of a coin is often the first thing potential buyers look at when evaluating its worth. Coins are typically graded on a scale that ranges from **poor** to **perfect**, with several grades in between. The most commonly used grading systems are the **Sheldon Scale** and the **American Numismatic Association (ANA)** guidelines. Familiarizing yourself with these grading systems will empower you to assess coins accurately and avoid overpaying for items that may not match their advertised condition.When examining a coin for grading, several **key factors** come into play. First, consider the **surface condition**. Look for any signs of wear, scratches, or blemishes. Coins that are well-preserved, with minimal marks, will typically receive higher grades. Next, assess the **strike** quality, which refers to how well the coin was struck during the minting process. A strong strike will show clear details and sharp edges, while a weak strike may appear blurry or lack definition.Another critical aspect of grading is the **luster** of the coin. Luster refers to the way light reflects off the coin's surface. A coin with a brilliant luster will have a shiny, reflective appearance, indicating that it has been well-preserved. On the other hand, a dull or matte appearance may suggest wear or improper storage conditions.Additionally, **color** plays a role in grading, especially for coins made from precious metals like gold and silver. Coins that retain their original color and toning are often more desirable than those that have been cleaned or altered. Cleaning can significantly reduce a coin's value, so it's essential to avoid any attempts to clean your coins yourself.

To further refine your grading skills, consider investing in a **magnifying glass** or a jeweler's loupe. These tools will allow you to examine coins in greater detail, helping you spot imperfections that may not be visible to the naked eye. Additionally, practice makes perfect; spend time comparing your coins to graded examples in reputable numismatic guides or online resources.As you gain experience, you may also want to familiarize yourself with the concept of **market grading**. This term refers to how coins are graded based on their marketability rather than strict adherence to grading standards. Market grading takes into account factors such as demand, rarity, and current market trends, which can influence a coin's perceived value.It's also important to understand that grading is somewhat subjective. Different graders may have varying opinions on a coin's condition, so it's wise to seek out multiple perspectives, especially when considering a significant purchase. Joining a local coin club or participating in online forums can provide valuable insights and help you develop a more nuanced understanding of coin grading.In summary, mastering coin grading is a vital skill for any collector. By understanding the key factors that influence a coin's grade and seeking out reliable resources, you'll be better equipped to make informed decisions and build a collection that you can proudly share with future generations. Remember, the journey of collecting is as much about the knowledge you gain as it is about the coins you acquire.

4. Starting Your Coin Collection

Starting your coin collection can be one of the most rewarding hobbies you embark on, combining history, art, and investment potential all in one. As you begin this journey, it's essential to approach it with a clear plan and an understanding of what you truly want to achieve. This chapter will guide you through the initial steps of building a collection that not only reflects your interests but also holds value over time.

Define Your Goals

Before you dive into the world of numismatics, take a moment to **define your goals**. Are you collecting for personal enjoyment, investment, or a combination of both? Understanding your motivation will help shape your collection. If you aim to create a collection that tells a story, think about the themes or historical periods that fascinate you. For instance, you might want to focus on ancient coins, coins from a specific country, or even coins that commemorate significant events.

Set a Budget

Establishing a **budget** is crucial. Coin collecting can range from affordable to extremely expensive, depending on the coins you choose. Determine how much you are willing to spend initially and on an ongoing basis. Remember, it's not just the purchase price of the coins that matters; consider storage, preservation supplies, and potential grading fees. A clear budget will help you make informed decisions and avoid overspending.

Research and Educate Yourself

Knowledge is power in coin collecting. Start by **researching reputable resources**—books, online forums, and websites dedicated to numismatics. Familiarize yourself with the basics of coin grading, types of coins, and market trends. Understanding the **value of coins** and how to identify them will enhance your confidence and help you make smarter purchases. Consider joining local coin clubs or attending shows to learn from experienced collectors.

Choose Your Focus

Once you have a grasp of your goals and budget, it's time to **choose a focus** for your collection. This could be anything from a specific coin series, like the U.S. state quarters, to a broader theme, such as world coins or coins from a particular era. Selecting a focus will not only make your collecting experience more enjoyable but will also help you develop expertise in that area.

Start Small

When beginning your collection, it's wise to **start small**. Look for coins that are affordable and easy to find. This approach allows you to learn the ropes without the pressure of high-stakes purchases. As you gain confidence and knowledge, you can gradually expand your collection to include more valuable or rare coins.

Buy from Reputable Sources

To avoid scams and counterfeit coins, always **buy from reputable sources**. This can include well-known dealers, coin shows, or established online platforms. Research the seller's reputation and look for reviews from other collectors. If possible, attend local coin shows to meet dealers in person and examine coins before making a purchase.

Document Your Collection

As you acquire coins, it's essential to **document your collection**. Keep a detailed record of each coin, including its purchase price, condition, and any relevant historical information. This documentation not only helps with organization but also provides valuable insight into your collection's growth and value over time.

Engage with the Community

Coin collecting is not just about the coins; it's also about the **community**. Engage with fellow collectors through online forums, social media groups, and local clubs. Sharing your experiences, asking questions, and learning from others can enhance your collecting journey. Plus, you'll have the opportunity to build lasting friendships with people who share your passion.

Preserve and Protect Your Coins

Proper **preservation** is vital to maintaining the value of your collection. Invest in quality storage solutions, such as coin holders, albums, or capsules that protect your coins from damage. Avoid handling coins with bare hands, as oils and dirt can cause harm. Instead, use cotton gloves when necessary and store your collection in a cool, dry place away from direct sunlight.

Enjoy the Journey

Lastly, remember that coin collecting is a journey, not just a destination. Take the time to enjoy the process of learning, discovering, and building your collection. Celebrate your milestones, whether it's acquiring a significant coin or simply mastering a new aspect of numismatics. This hobby is about more than just the coins; it's about the stories they tell and the memories you create along the way.

By following these steps, you'll be well on your way to building a rewarding and meaningful coin collection. Embrace the adventure, and let your passion for numismatics guide you as you embark on this exciting journey.

Setting Your Goals

Setting goals is a crucial first step in your coin collecting journey. Whether you're just starting out or looking to refine an existing collection, having clear objectives can guide your decisions and keep you motivated. Begin by asking yourself what you want to achieve with your collection. Are you aiming for historical significance, financial investment, or simply the joy of collecting? Identifying your primary motivation will shape your approach and help you stay focused.

Consider the Scope of Your Collection: Think about the types of coins that interest you the most. Are you drawn to ancient coins, modern issues, or specific themes like commemoratives or errors? Defining the scope of your collection can help you prioritize your purchases and prevent you from becoming overwhelmed by the vast array of options available.

Set a Budget: Financial planning is essential in coin collecting. Establish a budget that reflects your financial situation and collecting goals. This budget will guide your purchasing decisions and help you avoid overspending. Remember, it's not just about the initial purchase; consider ongoing costs like storage, insurance, and potential grading fees.

Define Your Timeline: Consider how much time you want to dedicate to your collecting hobby. Are you looking to build your collection quickly, or is this a long-term endeavor? Setting a timeline can help you manage your expectations and create a realistic plan for acquiring new pieces.

Document Your Progress: Keeping a record of your collection can enhance your experience. Documenting your acquisitions, including purchase dates, prices, and any relevant details about the coins, not only helps you track your investment but also adds a personal touch to your collection. Consider maintaining a digital or physical journal where you can reflect on your journey and the stories behind each coin.

Engage with the Community: Coin collecting is often more enjoyable when shared with others. Engaging with fellow collectors through local clubs or online forums can provide valuable insights and enhance your experience. Consider setting a goal to attend a certain number of shows or events each year to connect with others who share your passion.

Evaluate and Adjust: As you progress in your collecting journey, take time to evaluate your goals and adjust them as necessary. Your interests may evolve, or you might discover new areas of numismatics that capture your attention. Being flexible and open to change will In summary, setting clear goals in coin collecting is essential for a fulfilling and rewarding experience. By identifying your motivations, defining the scope of your collection, budgeting wisely, documenting your progress, engaging with the community, and remaining adaptable, you'll lay a strong foundation for your numismatic journey. Remember, the joy of collecting is not just in the coins themselves but in the stories they tell and the connections they foster.

Budgeting for Your Collection

When embarking on your coin collecting journey, one of the first and most crucial steps is **budgeting for your collection**. Establishing a clear financial plan not only helps you avoid overspending but also allows you to make informed decisions about which coins to acquire. Here's how to navigate this essential aspect of numismatics.Start by determining your **overall budget**. This should be a realistic figure based on your financial situation, taking into account your other obligations and savings goals. Consider how much you can comfortably allocate to your coin collection without jeopardizing your financial health. It's wise to set a specific amount that you can invest monthly or annually, which will help you stay disciplined and focused.

Next, think about **categories of coins** you're interested in collecting. Are you drawn to rare coins, historical pieces, or perhaps modern issues? Each category can have vastly different price ranges. By narrowing down your focus, you can allocate your budget more effectively. For example, if you decide to collect vintage coins, you might need to set aside a larger portion of your budget for fewer, higher-value items.Consider the **cost of additional expenses** associated with collecting. This includes not just the purchase price of coins, but also potential costs for grading, storage, insurance, and even travel to coin shows or auctions. These expenses can add up quickly, so it's essential to factor them into your overall budget to avoid surprises down the line.As you begin to build your collection, keep in mind the importance of **prioritizing purchases**. Not every coin you encounter will be a wise investment. Create a list of coins you want to acquire, ranking them based on your interests and their potential value. This will help you stay organized and focused, ensuring that you're making purchases that align with your collecting goals.Don't forget to leave room for **flexibility** in your budget. The world of coin collecting can be unpredictable, with unique opportunities arising unexpectedly. Whether it's a rare find at a local show or an auction that features a coin you've been eyeing, having a little extra budget can allow you to seize these moments without derailing your financial plan.

Another vital aspect of budgeting is to **track your expenses** meticulously. This not only helps you stay within your budget but also provides valuable insights into your collecting habits. Use a simple spreadsheet or a dedicated app to log each purchase, noting the date, price, and any additional costs. This practice will help you understand your spending patterns and adjust your budget as needed.As you refine your collecting strategy, consider the **potential for future value** in your collection. Some coins may appreciate significantly over time, while others may not hold their value as well. Research market trends and seek advice from reputable sources to make informed decisions about which coins to invest in. This foresight can help you build a collection that not only brings you joy but also serves as a valuable asset.Finally, remember that collecting should be **enjoyable**. While it's essential to be strategic and cautious with your finances, don't let budgeting become a burden. Allow yourself to appreciate the thrill of finding that perfect coin, and cherish the stories and history behind each piece in your collection. Balancing financial responsibility with the joy of collecting will ensure that your hobby remains fulfilling and rewarding.

Finding Coins: Sources and Strategies

Finding coins can be one of the most exhilarating aspects of numismatics. Whether you're a seasoned collector or just starting out, knowing where to look and how to strategize your search can significantly enhance your collection. Here are some effective sources and strategies to help you uncover those hidden treasures.

Local Coin Shops

Your first stop should be local coin shops. These establishments often have knowledgeable staff who can provide valuable insights into the coins they sell. **Building a relationship** with shop owners can lead to exclusive deals and first dibs on new arrivals. Don't hesitate to ask about their inventory turnover; shops that frequently update their stock may offer better chances of finding rare coins.

Coin Shows and Expos

Coin shows are a treasure trove for collectors. Attending these events allows you to interact with a variety of dealers and collectors, giving you a broader perspective on the market. **Networking** at these shows can also lead to future opportunities, such as private sales or insider tips on upcoming events. Make sure to carry cash, as many vendors prefer it over credit cards.

Online Marketplaces

The internet has revolutionized coin collecting. Websites like eBay, Etsy, and specialized numismatic sites offer a vast array of coins from different periods and regions. However, exercise caution— **authentication** is key when purchasing online. Always check seller ratings and reviews, and consider using payment methods that offer buyer protection.

Auctions

Participating in auctions can be thrilling, especially when bidding on coins that are hard to find elsewhere. Both online and in-person auctions provide access to unique items. Make sure to research the auction house's reputation and understand their terms before participating. **Set a budget** beforehand to avoid overspending in the heat of the moment.

Estate Sales and Flea Markets

Don't overlook estate sales and flea markets. These venues can yield unexpected finds, often at prices below market value. Approach these sales with an open mind and a keen eye. **Haggling** is often acceptable, so don't be shy about negotiating prices. You might just walk away with a rare coin that others missed.

Networking with Other Collectors

Join local coin clubs or online forums to connect with fellow collectors. These communities can provide leads on where to find coins and may even have members willing to sell or trade from their own collections. **Sharing knowledge** and experiences can greatly enhance your collecting journey and help you avoid common pitfalls.

Social Media

Platforms like Instagram and Facebook have become popular among numismatists. Many collectors showcase their finds and share tips on where to look. Follow reputable dealers and join groups dedicated to coin collecting. **Engagement** with these communities can lead to unique opportunities, such as private sales or trade offers.

Coin Books and Catalogs

Utilizing coin books and catalogs can be incredibly beneficial. They provide detailed information on various coins, including their history, market value, and rarity. Familiarize yourself with the **current market trends** by reading publications and guides, which will help you make informed decisions when sourcing coins.

Traveling to Historic Locations

If you have the opportunity, consider traveling to locations known for their historical significance in coinage. Museums, historical sites, and even foreign countries can provide unique insights and potential finds. **Exploring** these areas can also enhance your appreciation for the coins you collect.

Stay Informed

Finally, staying informed about the numismatic market is crucial. Subscribe to newsletters, join mailing lists, and follow industry news. Being aware of market fluctuations and upcoming releases can give you a competitive edge when searching for coins. **Knowledge is power** in this hobby, and the more you know, the better equipped you will be to find valuable additions to your collection.

In summary, finding coins requires a combination of strategy, networking, and knowledge. By utilizing local resources, engaging with the community, and staying informed, you can enhance your collecting experience and build a collection that you can proudly share with future generations.

Book 3: The World of U.S. Coinage

Understanding the world of U.S. coinage is essential for any collector, whether you're just starting out or have years of experience. The history, variety, and significance of these coins make them not only a fascinating hobby but also a potential investment. Here, we will delve into the key aspects of U.S. coinage that every collector should know.

Historical Overview

The story of U.S. coinage dates back to 1792 when the Coinage Act established the U.S. Mint. This act laid the groundwork for a national currency and set the stage for the diverse types of coins we see today. Over the years, various designs have emerged, reflecting the nation's history, culture, and values. **Understanding these historical contexts** can enhance your appreciation of the coins in your collection.

Types of U.S. Coins

U.S. coinage is categorized into several types, each with its unique characteristics. You have **circulating coins**, which are used in everyday transactions, and **numismatic coins**, which are collected for their rarity and historical significance. Among these, the most commonly collected include:

- **Pennies**: The one-cent coin, originally made of copper, has undergone various changes in composition and design.

- **Nickels**: The five-cent piece has a storied history, including designs featuring figures like Thomas Jefferson.

- **Dimes**: Worth ten cents, dimes have featured numerous designs, including the iconic Mercury dime.

- **Quarters**: Originally worth 25 cents, quarters have seen many designs, especially with the state quarters program.

- **Half Dollars**: These coins, worth 50 cents, often feature significant historical figures.

- **Dollars**: The most famous is the Eisenhower dollar, but there are many others worth exploring.   .

Coin Grading

Grading is a critical part of coin collecting and involves assessing a coin's condition and quality. The **Sheldon Scale** is commonly used, ranging from 1 (poor) to 70 (perfect). Understanding grading helps you determine a coin's value and authenticity. Familiarize yourself with terms like:

- **Uncirculated**: Coins that have never been used in transactions.

- **Proof**: Coins struck with higher quality for collectors, often with a mirror-like finish.

- **Mint State**: Coins that show no signs of wear.

Authentication Techniques

With the rise of counterfeiting, knowing how to authenticate coins is paramount. Techniques include:

- **Visual Inspection**: Look for inconsistencies in design, color, and weight.

- **Magnification**: Use a loupe to examine details that may reveal a counterfeit.

- **Weight and Measurement**: Authentic coins have specific weights and dimensions.

Consider investing in professional services for authentication if you're unsure.

Investing in U.S. Coins

Many collectors view their hobby as an investment opportunity. U.S. coins can appreciate in value over time, but it's essential to approach this aspect with caution. Research market trends and consider factors like **rarity**, **condition**, and **historical significance** when evaluating potential purchases. Diversifying your collection can also mitigate risks.

Community Engagement

Being part of the coin-collecting community can enhance your experience. Attend local coin shows, join clubs, or participate in online forums. These venues provide a wealth of knowledge and a chance to connect with fellow enthusiasts. Engaging with others can lead to valuable insights and opportunities for trading or purchasing coins.

Building a Legacy

Many collectors are motivated by the desire to pass down their collections. This goal can shape your collecting strategy. Consider documenting your collection's history and significance, creating a narrative that your children can appreciate. Involve them in the collecting process, teaching them about the coins and their stories. This shared experience can create lasting memories and instill a love for numismatics in future generations.

Exploring the world of U.S. coinage is a rewarding journey filled with history, artistry, and the potential for investment. By understanding the various types of coins, mastering grading and authentication techniques, and engaging with the community, you can build a collection that is not only valuable but also meaningful. Remember, each coin tells a story, and as a collector, you are its custodian

m

5. U.S. Coinage: A Historical Overview

The history of **U.S. coinage** is a fascinating journey that reflects the evolution of the nation itself. From the early days of colonial America, when coins were scarce and often imported, to the robust minting operations we see today, each era has left its mark on the coins we collect and cherish.

In the beginning, American colonists relied heavily on foreign coins, such as the **Spanish dollar**, which was widely accepted due to its silver content. The need for a uniform currency became apparent, leading to the establishment of the **U.S. Mint** in 1792. The first official coins produced were the **half dime**, **dime**, **quarter**, and **half dollar**. These coins were designed to represent the values and aspirations of a young nation, with symbols of liberty and democracy.

The introduction of the **penny** in 1793 marked a significant milestone in U.S. coinage. Initially made of copper, the penny underwent several design changes, including the iconic **Lincoln penny**, which has been in circulation since 1909. Each design reflects the artistic trends and cultural values of its time, showcasing figures such as **Lady Liberty** and **George Washington**.

As the nation grew, so did the complexity of its coinage. The **Gold Rush** of the mid-1800s spurred the minting of gold coins, including the famous **Double Eagle**, which became a symbol of wealth and prosperity. This era also saw the introduction of the **Seated Liberty** design, which featured a seated figure of Liberty on various denominations, emphasizing the nation's commitment to freedom and strength.

By the late 19th century, the **American numismatic landscape** underwent another transformation with the advent of the **Barber coinage**. Designed by Charles E. Barber, these coins were met with mixed reviews but remain popular among collectors today. The Barber series included the quarter, dime, and half-dollar, all featuring a classic design that has stood the test of time.

The turn of the 20th century brought about the **Indian Head penny** and the **Buffalo nickel**, both of which have become iconic representations of American culture. The Indian Head penny, with its depiction of a Native American, and the Buffalo nickel, showcasing the majestic bison, reflect the nation's diverse heritage and the importance of its natural resources.

As we moved into the mid-20th century, the **coinage system** faced challenges due to the economic upheaval of the Great Depression and World War II. The introduction of **silver coins** in the 1960s marked a significant change, as rising silver prices led to the gradual elimination of silver from circulating coins. The introduction of the **Washington quarter** and the **Kennedy half dollar** during this time became symbols of national pride and remembrance.

The 1970s and beyond saw the introduction of **clad coins**, which are composed of a core of a different metal, making them more affordable to produce. This transition allowed for the continued minting of coins while adapting to economic pressures. The design of coins also became more modern, with the introduction of the **State Quarters** program in 1999, which celebrated each state's unique history and culture.

Today, U.S. coinage continues to evolve, with the introduction of innovative designs and materials. The **American Innovation** series and the ongoing updates to the **Lincoln penny** and **Jefferson nickel** illustrate the ongoing commitment to honoring the past while embracing the future.

For collectors, understanding the historical context of U.S. coinage is crucial. Each coin tells a story, reflecting the values and events of its time. Whether you are a beginner or an advanced collector, appreciating the **rich history** behind these coins can enhance your collecting experience. As you build your collection, consider how each piece contributes to the broader narrative of American history, and remember that you are not just collecting coins but also preserving a part of the nation's legacy.

Colonial Coinage

Colonial coinage represents a fascinating chapter in the history of numismatics, reflecting the economic and political landscape of the time. As collectors, understanding the origins and significance of these coins can greatly enhance our appreciation and investment in this area.

The earliest coins used in the American colonies were often foreign coins, particularly those from Spain, England, and France. These coins circulated widely due to the lack of a standardized currency. **Spanish pieces of eight**, for instance, became a common choice, as they were universally recognized and trusted. The value of these coins was not just in their metal content but also in their acceptance among merchants and the general populace.

As the colonies grew, so did the need for a more localized currency. This led to the minting of colonial coins, a process that was often fraught with challenges. Each colony had its own economic needs and political motivations, which influenced the design and production of their coinage. For example, **Massachusetts** was among the first to produce its own coins in the 1650s, using a unique design that featured a pine tree, symbolizing the colony's natural resources and independence.

Another significant aspect of colonial coinage is the use of **tokens** and **paper money**. These were often issued by local merchants and governments as a stopgap measure to address the scarcity of coins. While these tokens were practical, they also introduced complexities into the market, as their value could fluctuate based on local demand and trust in the issuer. Collectors should be aware that many of these tokens are highly sought after today, often fetching high prices due to their rarity and historical significance.

Counterfeiting was a persistent issue during colonial times, just as it is today. Some enterprising individuals attempted to replicate popular coins, leading to a market filled with fakes. Understanding how to identify genuine colonial coins is crucial for any collector. Look for **distinctive markings**, variations in weight, and the quality of craftsmanship. Engaging with experts and utilizing reliable resources can significantly reduce the risk of falling victim to counterfeit coins.

The role of colonial coinage extends beyond mere currency; it also serves as a reflection of the sociopolitical climate of the time. Coins often bore images of monarchs, symbols of the colonies, or inscriptions that conveyed messages of loyalty, independence, or economic strength. For instance, coins minted during the Revolutionary War featured patriotic themes, embodying the spirit of the struggle for independence. Collectors should consider the historical context of each coin, as this can enhance its value and significance in a collection.

When building a collection of colonial coins, it's essential to focus on quality over quantity. A well-curated collection, featuring a few high-quality pieces, can be more valuable and meaningful than a large assortment of lesser-quality coins. Pay attention to the **grade** of each coin, as this will significantly impact its market value. Familiarize yourself with grading standards and seek out coins that are in good condition, as these will stand the test of time and maintain their value.

Engaging with fellow collectors can also enhance your understanding of colonial coinage. Local coin shows, online forums, and numismatic clubs provide opportunities to share knowledge, trade coins, and gain insights from experienced collectors. This community aspect can be particularly rewarding, as it fosters connections and a shared passion for the hobby.

As you delve into the world of colonial coinage, consider the legacy you wish to create. These coins are not just historical artifacts; they are tangible connections to our past. Sharing your collection with family can instill a sense of history and appreciation for numismatics in future generations. Involving children or grandchildren in your collecting journey can create lasting memories and a shared interest that transcends time.

In summary, colonial coinage offers a rich tapestry of history, artistry, and economic significance. As you navigate this fascinating field, prioritize authenticity, engage with the community, and focus on building a collection that tells a story. Remember, each coin is a piece of history, and understanding its background can greatly enhance your enjoyment and investment in this rewarding hobby.

Early American Coinage (1792-1830)

In the early years of the United States, the fledgling nation faced the challenge of establishing a cohesive monetary system. The Coinage Act of 1792 marked a significant milestone, as it led to the creation of the United States Mint and the introduction of the first federal coins. This period was characterized by a mix of colonial influences and the need for a uniquely American currency, setting the stage for a rich numismatic history.

The first coins produced by the U.S. Mint were the **half dismes** and **dimes**, minted in 1792. These coins were initially struck in silver and represented a crucial step toward standardizing currency across the nation. The half disme, although not widely circulated, is particularly sought after by collectors today due to its rarity and historical significance.

As the Mint began producing larger denominations, the **flowing hair** design of the coins became iconic. The **flowing hair dollar**, introduced in 1794, was one of the first silver dollars minted by the U.S. This coin features a beautiful depiction of Liberty, with flowing hair symbolizing freedom and the spirit of the new nation. Collectors value these coins not only for their artistry but also for their historical context.

The early 19th century saw the introduction of the **draped bust** design, which replaced the flowing hair motif. The draped bust coins, minted from 1796 to 1807, include various denominations such as the half dollar and the dollar. These coins are characterized by their more formal representation of Liberty, draped in a classical style. The draped bust dollar is particularly notable for its striking design and rarity, making it a prized possession for many collectors.

In 1804, the Mint produced a small number of **1804 dollars** that would later become one of the most famous and sought-after coins in American numismatic history. These coins were not actually minted in 1804 but were produced later for presentation purposes. The legend of the 1804 dollar is rich with intrigue and has captivated collectors for generations, with some specimens fetching millions at auction.

As the nation expanded, so did its coinage. The introduction of the **Capped Bust** design in 1807 brought a new aesthetic to American coins. This design remained in use through the 1830s and included various denominations, including the quarter and half dollar. The Capped Bust coins are celebrated for their detailed engravings and are a testament to the evolving artistry of American coinage.

Throughout this period, the Mint faced challenges, including the need to combat counterfeiting. As coin collecting began to gain popularity, the threat of counterfeit coins emerged. Collectors during this time needed to be vigilant, as many forgeries circulated in the marketplace. Understanding the nuances of early American coinage is crucial for any collector aiming to build a historically significant collection.

In addition to the designs and denominations, the early American coinage era also introduced various mint marks, which denote where a coin was produced. The Philadelphia Mint was the primary mint during this time, but other locations, such as the New Orleans Mint, began operations later, adding another layer of complexity to coin collecting. Mint marks can significantly affect a coin's value and rarity, making them an essential consideration for collectors.

As collectors delve into early American coinage, they should pay close attention to the **condition** of the coins. The grading of coins from this period can be subjective, and factors such as wear, luster, and the presence of any marks or blemishes can influence a coin's value. Beginners should familiarize themselves with grading standards to avoid potential pitfalls when purchasing coins.

Moreover, understanding the historical context behind each coin can enhance a collector's appreciation for their collection. Many early coins are tied to significant events in American history, such as the War of 1812 or the Louisiana Purchase. These connections not only enrich the narrative of the collection but also create opportunities for collectors to share their passion with family and friends, fostering a deeper connection to the hobby.

In conclusion, the early American coinage period from 1792 to 1830 lays a solid foundation for any collector interested in numismatics. The blend of artistry, history, and the evolution of currency provides a captivating journey for those who choose to explore it. By focusing on authenticity, understanding the significance of mint marks, and appreciating the historical narratives behind each coin, collectors can build a collection that is not only valuable but also meaningful—a legacy to be shared with future generations.

Modern Coinage (Post-1830 to Present)

The evolution of modern coinage from post-1830 to the present is a fascinating journey that reflects not only economic changes but also cultural shifts and technological advancements. This period marks a significant transition in how coins are designed, minted, and perceived by collectors and the public alike.

Historical Context

By the early 19th century, the industrial revolution was in full swing, leading to increased demand for currency that could support growing economies. **Governments began to standardize coinage**, resulting in a more uniform approach to minting that would lay the groundwork for modern monetary systems. The establishment of national mints and the introduction of new metals, such as nickel and bronze, further diversified the coinage landscape.

Design Innovations

Modern coinage is characterized by **innovative designs** that often reflect national identity, historical events, and cultural symbols. The introduction of the **Seated Liberty design** in the United States during the 1830s exemplifies this trend. Artists like Augustus Saint-Gaudens and Adolph Weinman later contributed iconic designs, such as the **Saint-Gaudens Double Eagle** and the **Mercury Dime**, which remain highly sought after by collectors today.

Technological Advancements

Advancements in minting technology have drastically changed the production of coins. The introduction of steam-powered machinery in the 19th century allowed for **mass production** of coins, making them more accessible to the public. Additionally, the use of **laser technology** and computer-aided design in recent decades has enabled the creation of intricate designs and improved the accuracy of coin production.

Collecting Trends

The modern era has seen a surge in coin collecting, driven by both hobbyists and investors. The rise of the internet has facilitated access to information and marketplaces, allowing collectors to connect globally. **Specialized collecting** has become more popular, with enthusiasts focusing on specific themes, such as commemorative coins, error coins, or coins from particular historical periods.

Investment Potential

For many, coin collecting is not just a hobby but also an investment strategy. The **value of rare coins** has appreciated significantly over the years, often outperforming traditional investments like stocks and bonds. Understanding market trends, grading standards, and the factors that contribute to a coin's value is essential for collectors looking to build a financially rewarding collection.

Counterfeits and Authentication

As the popularity of coin collecting has grown, so too has the prevalence of **counterfeit coins**. This underscores the importance of authentication and education. Collectors must equip themselves with the knowledge to identify genuine coins versus fakes. Resources such as professional grading services and authentication guides can help mitigate the risk of purchasing counterfeits and ensure that collectors make informed decisions.

Global Perspectives

While much of the focus in modern coinage has been on North America, it is crucial to recognize the global landscape. Countries around the world have developed unique coinage systems, influenced by their own histories and cultures. **International coin collecting** offers a rich tapestry of options for collectors, from ancient coins to contemporary issues, providing an opportunity to explore diverse numismatic traditions.

Legacy and Family Involvement

One of the most rewarding aspects of coin collecting is the ability to pass down knowledge and collections to future generations. Engaging family members in the hobby can create lasting memories and foster an appreciation for history and culture. **Encouraging children** to participate in coin collecting can instill valuable lessons about finance, history, and the importance of preserving heritage.

Modern coinage represents a dynamic intersection of art, history, and economics. For collectors, understanding the evolution of coins from post-1830 to the present is essential not only for building a valuable collection but also for appreciating the broader context of their hobby. As you navigate this exciting world, remember to seek reliable information, engage with the community, and enjoy the journey of discovery that coin collecting offers.

Book 4: Exploring Global Coinage

Coin collecting is a global hobby that transcends borders, cultures, and languages. Each country has its own unique history, economy, and artistry reflected in its coinage. As you delve into the world of global coinage, you'll find a rich tapestry of stories, traditions, and innovations that can enhance your collection and deepen your appreciation for numismatics.

Understanding the Cultural Context

Coins are more than just currency; they are a reflection of a nation's identity. When collecting international coins, it's essential to understand the **cultural significance** behind them. For example, the intricate designs on Indian rupees often depict deities or historical figures, showcasing the country's rich heritage. Similarly, the **Euro** coins feature designs that celebrate the collective history of Europe, emphasizing unity and diversity. Exploring these cultural contexts not only enriches your collection but also connects you to the stories behind each coin.

Identifying Rare International Coins

As you expand your collection to include international coins, you may encounter **rare varieties** that pique your interest. Some coins are produced in limited quantities or are only available in specific regions. For instance, the **Australian Kookaburra** series is highly sought after by collectors for its changing designs each year. Understanding how to identify these rare coins, including their **mint marks** and production numbers, is crucial for building a valuable collection.

Investment Potential of Global Coins

Investing in international coins can be a lucrative venture, but it requires careful consideration. The **global coin market** is influenced by various factors, including economic stability, collector demand, and geopolitical events. Coins from emerging markets may offer significant growth potential, but they also come with increased risk. Researching trends and understanding the **investment landscape** of different countries can help you make informed decisions and potentially enhance the value of your collection over time.

Authentication and Avoiding Counterfeits

As with any collecting endeavor, the risk of encountering counterfeits rises when dealing with international coins. Each country has its own methods for minting and authenticating coins, which can make it challenging to determine authenticity. Familiarize yourself with **authentication techniques** specific to the countries you are collecting from. Resources such as guides, forums, and professional appraisers can provide invaluable insights into identifying genuine coins and avoiding scams.

Building a Diverse Collection

A well-rounded coin collection includes a variety of coins from different regions and eras. Consider focusing on specific themes, such as **historical events**, notable figures, or unique designs. This thematic approach not only enhances your collection but also allows you to share fascinating stories with family and friends. Engaging your children in the process can create lasting memories and instill a passion for history and collecting.

Connecting with Global Collectors

Joining international numismatic communities can provide you with a wealth of knowledge and resources. Online forums, social media groups, and local coin clubs often host discussions about global coinage, allowing you to connect with fellow collectors. Participating in these communities can lead to valuable exchanges of information, tips on where to find rare coins, and even opportunities to trade or sell pieces from your collection.

Resources for Global Coin Collecting

To successfully navigate the world of global coinage, you'll need reliable resources. Books, websites, and databases dedicated to international numismatics can serve as essential tools for research and authentication. Look for publications that specialize in global coins, providing detailed descriptions, images, and market analyses. Additionally, attending **international coin shows** can expose you to a variety of coins and connect you with experts in the field.

Preserving Your Collection

Proper care and preservation of your coins are vital to maintaining their condition and value. This is especially true for international coins, which may be more susceptible to environmental damage. Use **protective holders** or albums specifically designed for coins to prevent scratches and tarnishing.

Additionally, store your collection in a controlled environment, away from direct sunlight and humidity, to ensure its longevity.

Legacy and Family Involvement

As you build your collection, consider how you can involve your family in the process. Sharing the excitement of discovering new coins or learning about their history can create a meaningful bond. Encourage your children to participate in coin shows or help with research, fostering a sense of **legacy** and appreciation for the hobby. By passing down your knowledge and passion for coin collecting, you'll create lasting memories and inspire the next generation.

Exploring global coinage opens up a world of possibilities for collectors. By understanding the cultural context, identifying rare coins, and connecting with fellow enthusiasts, you can enhance your collection and enjoy the journey of numismatics. Remember, each coin tells a story, and as you expand your horizons, you'll discover a rich narrative waiting to be uncovered.

6. World Coinage: Going Global

When diving into the realm of **world coinage**, collectors are opened up to a vast array of cultures, histories, and currencies. Each country has its own unique story told through its coins, reflecting the values, achievements, and even the struggles of its people. This chapter will guide you through the essential aspects of collecting international coins, emphasizing the importance of understanding context and authenticity.

One of the first steps in world coin collecting is recognizing the **historical significance** of the coins you encounter. Coins are not just currency; they are artifacts that provide insight into the era they were minted. For instance, coins from ancient Rome can tell you about the political climate, trade routes, and even daily life during that period. Similarly, modern coins can reflect a nation's identity, commemorative events, or pivotal moments in history. Understanding the **background** of a coin enhances its value, both financially and sentimentally.

As you begin to expand your collection beyond North America, it's crucial to familiarize yourself with the **different coin systems** used around the world. Many countries have unique denominations, materials, and designs that can be vastly different from what you may be accustomed to. For example, the Euro, which is used by multiple European countries, features a variety of national designs on one side, while the reverse side remains consistent across all nations. This diversity can be fascinating and adds depth to your collection.

When collecting world coins, **authenticity** becomes a paramount concern. Counterfeit coins are prevalent in the market, and distinguishing genuine pieces from fakes requires a keen eye and some knowledge. Familiarize yourself with the specific characteristics of coins from different countries, including mint marks, weight, and dimensions. Utilizing resources such as **authentication services** or reputable dealers can also help ensure that your collection is composed of genuine articles. Remember, investing in a coin is not just about its aesthetic appeal; it's about acquiring a piece of history.

Another exciting aspect of world coin collecting is the **opportunity to connect** with other collectors and experts globally. Engaging in online forums or attending international coin shows can provide valuable insights and knowledge sharing. These platforms often feature discussions about trends in world coin collecting, tips for spotting counterfeits, and recommendations for reputable dealers. Building a network can also lead to potential trades or purchases that might not be available locally.

As you explore various international coins, consider the **cultural significance** behind them. Many coins feature national symbols, historical figures, or events that are important to their respective countries. For instance, coins from Japan often showcase designs that reflect traditional arts, while coins from South Africa might highlight the nation's wildlife. Understanding these cultural elements not only enriches your collecting experience but also allows you to appreciate the stories behind each coin.

When it comes to **storage and care** of your world coins, it's essential to treat them with respect. Use appropriate holders or albums designed for coin storage to prevent damage. Avoid cleaning coins, as this can significantly decrease their value. Instead, if you encounter dirt or tarnish, consult a professional conservator who specializes in numismatics. Proper care will ensure that your collection remains in excellent condition for years to come.

For those interested in **investing** in world coins, understanding market trends is crucial. The value of coins can fluctuate based on demand, rarity, and historical context. Researching auction results, attending coin shows, and following reputable numismatic publications can help you stay informed about the market. Additionally, consider diversifying your collection by including coins from emerging markets or those with increasing popularity among collectors.

Finally, as you build your world coin collection, think about how you want to **share this passion** with future generations. Documenting your collection with detailed notes about each coin's origin, significance, and personal stories can create a wonderful legacy for your children. Involving them in the collecting process can also foster a shared interest in history and culture, making it a rewarding family activity.

In conclusion, world coinage offers a rich tapestry of history, culture, and investment potential. By understanding the significance of the coins you collect, ensuring their authenticity, and engaging with the global community of collectors, you can create a collection that is not only valuable but also deeply meaningful. Whether you're drawn to the stories behind the coins or the thrill of the hunt, the world of numismatics awaits you with open arms.

Ancient Coins

Ancient coins represent a fascinating intersection of history, art, and economics, providing collectors with a tangible connection to the past. The allure of these coins often lies in the stories they tell about the civilizations that minted them. From the intricate designs to the historical significance, ancient coins can be both a rewarding investment and a captivating hobby.

Understanding Ancient Coinage

Ancient coins were typically made from precious metals like gold, silver, and bronze, and their designs often featured the rulers, deities, or symbols significant to the culture. The value of these coins is not only in their metal content but also in their rarity and historical context. Collectors should familiarize themselves with major ancient civilizations, such as the Greek, Roman, and Byzantine empires, as each offers unique coins with distinct characteristics.

Key Characteristics

When assessing ancient coins, collectors should pay attention to several key characteristics:

- **Material:** Ancient coins were made from various metals, and understanding the metal composition can help determine authenticity and value.
- **Design:** Coins often feature intricate designs that can indicate the period and region of origin. Familiarity with common motifs can aid in identification.
- **Condition:** The state of preservation significantly impacts a coin's value. Terms like Fine, Very Fine, and Extremely Fine are commonly used to describe condition.
- **Provenance:** The history of ownership can add value. Coins with a well-documented provenance are often more desirable.

Authentication Techniques

One of the primary concerns for collectors is ensuring the authenticity of ancient coins. Counterfeiting has been a challenge in numismatics for centuries, and modern technology has made it easier to produce convincing fakes. Here are some techniques to help authenticate ancient coins:

- **Visual Inspection:** Look for irregularities in design, weight, and patina. Genuine ancient coins often have wear that reflects their age.
- **Weight and Size:** Accurate measurements can help identify discrepancies. Most ancient coins have standard weights and sizes that can be referenced.
- **Professional Grading:** Consider sending coins to a reputable grading service for a professional opinion. This can provide added assurance of authenticity.

Investment Potential

Investing in ancient coins can be both rewarding and lucrative. The market for ancient coins has shown resilience over the years, often appreciating in value due to their historical significance and rarity. However, it's crucial to approach this investment with care:

- **Diversify Your Collection:** Just as with any investment, diversification can mitigate risk. Consider collecting coins from various periods and regions.
- **Research Market Trends:** Stay informed about market trends and auction results to understand which coins are gaining popularity.
- **Build Relationships:** Engage with dealers and fellow collectors to gain insights and advice. Networking can lead to valuable opportunities.

Building a Legacy

For many collectors, the goal extends beyond personal enjoyment; it includes creating a legacy to share with future generations. Here are some ways to involve your family in the hobby:

- **Education:** Teach your children about the history behind the coins. This can foster an appreciation for history and art.
- **Involvement:** Include them in the collecting process, from attending shows to researching coins together.
- **Documentation:** Maintain a record of the collection, including notes on each coin's history and significance. This can serve as a valuable resource for future generations.

European Coins

When diving into the world of European coins, collectors are greeted with a rich tapestry of history, culture, and artistry. The diversity of coinage across the continent reflects not only the various nations but also the evolution of monetary systems through the ages.

Historical Significance: Each European coin tells a story. From the ancient Roman denarius to the modern euro, these coins have witnessed the rise and fall of empires, the spread of Christianity, and the intricate dance of trade and commerce. Understanding the historical context of a coin can significantly enhance its value and appeal to collectors.

Types of Coins: European coinage is incredibly varied. You can find everything from ancient coins, like Greek drachmas and Roman sestertii, to modern commemorative coins celebrating significant events or figures. Each type offers a unique glimpse into the culture and values of its time. Collectors often focus on specific eras, such as the Middle Ages or the Renaissance, which can provide a more structured approach to building a collection.

Authentication Techniques: Given the prevalence of counterfeits, particularly in the European market, it's crucial for collectors to develop robust authentication skills. Familiarizing oneself with the characteristics of genuine coins, such as weight, diameter, and design details, is essential. Resources like the **World Coin Price Guide** can be invaluable in determining a coin's authenticity and market value.

Investment Potential: European coins can serve as a sound investment. Coins from certain historical periods, especially those in excellent condition, can appreciate significantly over time. Collectors should research market trends and seek advice from reputable dealers to make informed purchasing decisions. Additionally, understanding the economic conditions of the countries of origin can provide insight into future value.

Community Engagement: Joining local or online numismatic societies can enrich the collecting experience. Engaging with fellow collectors allows for the sharing of knowledge, resources, and experiences. Many clubs host coin shows, workshops, and seminars, providing opportunities for hands-on learning and networking.

Preservation and Care: Proper care and preservation of European coins are essential to maintaining their condition and value. Coins should be stored in a controlled environment, away from moisture and extreme temperatures. Using appropriate holders or albums can prevent physical damage and tarnishing. Regularly inspecting your collection for signs of wear or deterioration is also advisable.

Famous Collections: Throughout history, several notable collections have made headlines, showcasing the allure of European coins. The **British Museum** houses an extensive collection that spans thousands of years, while private collectors have amassed remarkable troves that highlight the beauty and significance of these pieces. Learning about these collections can inspire new collectors and provide insights into what makes certain coins desirable.

Global Influence: European coins have had a profound impact on global currency systems. The introduction of the euro, for instance, has transformed the economic landscape of Europe and beyond. Understanding the implications of such changes can help collectors appreciate the broader significance of their collections.

Future Trends: As the numismatic world evolves, staying informed about emerging trends in coin collecting is crucial. Digital currencies and the rise of online marketplaces are reshaping how collectors buy and sell coins. Keeping an eye on these developments can provide collectors with new opportunities and insights into the future of their hobby.

In conclusion, collecting European coins is not just about acquiring currency; it's about embracing a rich historical narrative and becoming part of a global community. With careful research, a focus on authenticity, and a passion for sharing knowledge, collectors can build meaningful collections that stand the test of time.

Asian Coins

Asian coins have a rich and diverse history that reflects the vast cultures and economies of the continent. From ancient times to modern-day, these coins tell stories of trade, power, and artistry.

Collecting Asian coins can be both a rewarding and educational endeavor, allowing collectors to explore the intricate designs and historical significance behind each piece.

Historical Significance

The history of Asian coins dates back thousands of years, with some of the earliest examples originating in China. The **Chinese cash coins**, characterized by their round shape with a square hole in the center, were used for centuries and symbolize the long-standing tradition of coinage in Asia. Other regions, such as India, Japan, and Southeast Asia, also have unique coinage histories that reflect their respective cultures and economies. Understanding the historical context of these coins can enhance your appreciation and knowledge as a collector.

Types of Asian Coins

When it comes to Asian coins, there is a vast array of types to explore. Some notable categories include:

- **Chinese Coins:** These include ancient cash coins, silver and gold ingots, as well as modern commemorative issues.

- **Japanese Yen:** The yen has undergone various changes since its inception, with many collectors focusing on rare editions and historical notes.

- **Indian Coins:** From ancient punch-marked coins to the British Raj issues, Indian coins showcase a rich tapestry of history.

- **Southeast Asian Coins:** Countries like Thailand, Vietnam, and Indonesia have their own unique coinage, often influenced by trade and colonial history.

Collecting Tips

As you delve into collecting Asian coins, there are several tips to keep in mind:

- **Research:** Familiarize yourself with the different types of coins, their historical significance, and common counterfeits. Knowledge is your best defense against scams.
- **Condition Matters:** Pay attention to the condition of the coins. Grading can significantly impact value, so understanding how to assess a coin's condition is crucial.
- **Authenticity:** Always seek to verify the authenticity of coins before making a purchase. Utilize reputable dealers and consider professional grading services.
- **Networking:** Engage with fellow collectors through forums and local coin shows. Building a community can provide support and valuable insights.

Investment Potential

Investing in Asian coins can be a lucrative venture if approached wisely. The demand for rare and historically significant coins continues to grow, making them an attractive option for collectors and investors alike. However, it's essential to stay informed about market trends and potential risks.Consider focusing on **historically significant coins** or those with unique stories behind them. Coins that are tied to important events or figures often appreciate in value over time.

Preserving Your Collection

Proper preservation of your Asian coin collection is vital to maintaining its value. Here are some practices to consider:

- **Storage:** Store coins in a cool, dry place away from direct sunlight. Use protective holders or capsules to prevent damage.
- **Handling:** Always handle coins by the edges to avoid fingerprints and oils from your skin, which can cause damage over time.
- **Documentation:** Keep a detailed record of your collection, including purchase dates, prices, and any relevant historical information.

Engaging with Family

Sharing your passion for numismatics with your children can create lasting memories and a sense of legacy. Teach them about the history behind each coin, and encourage them to start their own collections. This not only enriches their understanding of history but also fosters a deeper appreciation for the art of coin collecting.Collecting Asian coins offers a unique opportunity to explore the rich tapestry of history and culture that these coins represent. By focusing on authenticity, staying informed, and engaging with your community, you can build a meaningful collection that not only serves as a valuable investment but also as a cherished legacy to pass down to future generations.

Coins from Oceania, Africa, and the Americans

Coin collecting is a fascinating journey that spans across continents, and the coins from Oceania, Africa, and the Americas showcase a rich tapestry of history and culture. Each region offers unique insights into their societies through their coinage, making them not just collectibles but also an avenue for learning and connection.

Oceania: A Mosaic of Cultures

The coins from Oceania reflect a diverse array of cultures, languages, and traditions. Countries like Australia and New Zealand have coins that are not only used for everyday transactions but also serve as a canvas for indigenous art and significant historical events. The **Australian Kangaroo** and the **New Zealand Kiwi** are prime examples of how national symbols are celebrated through coin design.

In addition to these modern coins, collectors should also pay attention to the **Pacific Islands' currencies**. Many islands have their own unique designs and denominations, often featuring local wildlife or cultural symbols. Understanding the context behind these coins can enhance your appreciation and value of your collection.

Africa: A Rich Heritage

African coins are steeped in history, often telling stories of ancient civilizations and colonial influences. Countries like South Africa and Egypt offer coins that are not only beautiful but also historically significant. The **Krugerrand**, for instance, is famous for its gold content and has become a staple for investors and collectors alike.

Moreover, many African nations have recently minted coins that celebrate their independence and cultural heritage. Coins featuring **African wildlife**, traditional attire, and historical figures are becoming increasingly popular among collectors. It's essential to research the historical significance of these coins, as they often reflect the nation's journey and identity.

The Americas: From Ancient Civilizations to Modern Minting

The Americas boast a rich numismatic history, from the ancient coins of the Aztecs and Incas to the modern-day currencies of the United States and Canada. The **United States Mint** has produced a wide variety of coins that appeal to collectors, including commemorative issues and limited editions.

In addition to U.S. coins, Canadian coins are also noteworthy, particularly those that incorporate **indigenous art** and themes. The Royal Canadian Mint has been known for its innovative designs and high-quality production, making Canadian coins a valuable addition to any collection.

Furthermore, Latin American countries have a wealth of historical coins that reflect their colonial past and indigenous cultures. Coins from Mexico, for example, often feature the **Mexican Eagle** and other symbols that are deeply rooted in the nation's heritage. Collectors should take the time to explore these coins, as they can provide a deeper understanding of the region's history.

Investing and Collecting Tips

When collecting coins from Oceania, Africa, and the Americas, it's crucial to keep a few key considerations in mind. First, always verify the **authenticity** of the coins you are purchasing. Given the potential for counterfeits, particularly in regions with a high volume of collectors, having a reliable authentication guide is invaluable.

Additionally, consider the **market trends** for specific coins. Researching recent sales, auction results, and collector interest can help you make informed decisions about which coins to add to your collection. Joining online forums or local coin clubs can also provide insights from experienced collectors who can share their knowledge and experiences.

Preserving Your Collection

Proper preservation techniques are vital to maintaining the value of your coins. Store them in a cool, dry place and use protective holders to prevent damage. Avoid cleaning coins, as this can significantly decrease their value. Instead, focus on displaying them in a way that protects their condition while allowing you to enjoy your collection.

Finally, as you build your collection, think about the legacy you wish to leave behind. Involving your family in your hobby can create lasting memories and instill a love for numismatics in the next generation. Share stories about your coins, their significance, and the adventures you've had in acquiring them. This not only enriches your collecting experience but also creates a bond that can be passed down through your family.

Book 5: Identifying and Collecting Specific Coins

Coin collecting is a fascinating journey, and understanding the nuances of specific coins can elevate your collection from ordinary to extraordinary. Whether you're drawn to the allure of ancient coins, the artistry of modern minting, or the historical significance of commemorative pieces, recognizing what makes each coin unique is essential for every collector.

Understanding Coin Types

Each coin type tells a story, and knowing the differences can enhance your appreciation. For instance, **ancient coins** often feature intricate designs that reflect the culture and era from which they originated. **Modern coins**, on the other hand, might showcase technological advancements in minting and design. Familiarizing yourself with various types, such as **gold, silver, and copper coins**, is crucial for any collector.

Recognizing Key Features

When assessing a coin, focus on its **key features**. These include the coin's **mint mark**, **year of issue**, and **design elements**. Each of these can significantly affect a coin's value and desirability. For example, a rare mint mark can indicate limited production, making that coin more sought after. Additionally, understanding **die varieties** can reveal unique characteristics that add to a coin's story.

Condition and Grading

The condition of a coin is paramount in determining its value. Coins are graded based on their **physical appearance**, which includes factors such as **wear, luster, and surface quality**. Familiarizing yourself with the **Sheldon scale** (ranging from 1 to 70) will help you communicate effectively with other collectors and dealers. Remember, a coin in better condition can command a significantly higher price.

Authentication Techniques

With the prevalence of counterfeit coins, being able to authenticate your pieces is essential. Learn to use tools such as a **magnifying glass** or a **digital microscope** to inspect fine details. Look for **specific markers** that can indicate authenticity, such as the texture of the coin's surface or the precision of the engraving. Additionally, consider seeking third-party grading services for a professional opinion.

Researching Historical Context

Understanding the historical context of the coins you collect can deepen your connection to them. Each coin has a story, often tied to significant events, figures, or cultural shifts. For example, collecting **commemorative coins** can provide insights into the events they celebrate. Engaging with resources such as **numismatic journals** or **online databases** can enhance your knowledge and appreciation.

Building Your Collection

When building your collection, consider focusing on a specific theme or era. This could be anything from **ancient Roman coins** to **20th-century American currency**. A focused collection not only enhances the value of your holdings but also makes your collecting experience more fulfilling. Additionally, think about how you want to display your collection; presentation can significantly impact the perceived value of your coins.

Community Engagement

Engaging with the numismatic community can enrich your collecting experience. Attend **local coin shows** to meet fellow collectors and dealers. Online forums can also be invaluable for sharing knowledge and experiences. Platforms like **Reddit** or specialized numismatic websites can provide a wealth of information and support.

Investing in Your Collection

As you build your collection, consider the investment potential of your coins. While collecting should primarily be about passion, understanding market trends can help you make informed decisions. Keep an eye on **auction results** and **price guides** to gauge the value of your coins. Remember, investing in numismatics can be rewarding, but it requires careful research and patience.

Passing Down Your Collection

One of the most rewarding aspects of coin collecting is the opportunity to pass your collection down to future generations. Share your knowledge with your children or family members, and involve them in the collecting process. This not only helps preserve your legacy but also fosters a love for history and collecting in the next generation.

Final Thoughts

Collecting specific coins is not merely about acquiring pieces; it's about understanding their significance and the stories they tell. By focusing on the details, engaging with the community, and embracing the journey, you can build a collection that is both valuable and meaningful. Remember, every coin has a history, and it's up to you to uncover and share it.

7. Identifying Coin Types and Series

When starting your journey into coin collecting, understanding the various **types and series** of coins is essential. This knowledge not only enhances your appreciation of numismatics but also aids in making informed decisions when purchasing or trading coins. Each coin type has its unique characteristics, historical significance, and appeal to collectors, making it crucial to familiarize yourself with them.

Understanding Coin Types

Coins can be categorized into several types based on their characteristics, such as design, denomination, and issuing authority. The most common types include:

- **Circulating Coins:** These are the coins you see in daily transactions. They are produced in large quantities and are often less valuable than collectible coins.

- **Commemorative Coins:** Issued to honor a specific event, person, or anniversary, these coins are typically produced in limited quantities and can be more valuable.

- **Proof Coins:** Struck with a special process to create a mirror-like finish, proof coins are often sought after by collectors for their aesthetic appeal.

- **Mint Errors:** Coins that have been produced with mistakes during the minting process. These unique pieces can be highly sought after by collectors.

Exploring Coin Series

Within each type, you will find various **series** that reflect different historical periods or themes. Understanding these series can help you identify what makes a coin collectible. Here are a few notable series:

- **Lincoln Cent Series:** This series, which began in 1909, features various designs and mint marks, making it a popular choice among collectors.

- **American Silver Eagle:** Introduced in 1986, this series is known for its silver content and iconic design, appealing to both investors and collectors.

- **State Quarters:** Minted between 1999 and 2008, this series celebrates each state in the U.S. and has captured the interest of many new collectors.

- **Buffalo Nickel Series:** Produced from 1913 to 1938, these coins are appreciated for their artistic design and historical significance.

Recognizing Historical Context

Each coin type and series has its own **historical context**, which can greatly influence its value and desirability. Learning about the events or figures depicted on the coins can provide deeper insights into their significance. For example, the **Walking Liberty Half Dollar** not only represents a beautiful design but also reflects the spirit of American resilience during the early 20th century.

Condition and Grading

The condition of a coin plays a pivotal role in its value. Understanding how to assess the **grade** of a coin is essential for collectors. Coins are graded on a scale from 1 to 70, with higher numbers indicating better condition. Familiarizing yourself with grading standards can help you determine the authenticity and potential value of your collection.

Engaging with Coin Communities

As you delve deeper into the world of coin collecting, consider joining **coin clubs** or online forums. These communities provide valuable resources for learning about different coin types and series, as well as opportunities to connect with fellow collectors. Engaging with others can enhance your understanding and appreciation of numismatics.

Building Your Collection

When building your collection, focus on **diversity** by including various types and series. This approach not only makes your collection more interesting but also increases its potential value over time. As you gain more knowledge, you may even discover niche areas that resonate with your collecting style.

Final Thoughts

Identifying coin types and series is the first step in your collecting journey. By understanding the different categories and their historical significance, you can make informed decisions and build a collection that reflects your interests and values. Remember, the world of numismatics is vast and ever-evolving, so stay curious and engaged as you explore this fascinating hobby.

Half Cents and Cents

When it comes to **half cents and cents**, collectors often find themselves drawn into a rich history that reflects the economic and social changes of their times. These coins are not just currency; they embody stories of a nation's evolution. Understanding these coins requires a blend of historical knowledge, market insight, and an appreciation for the artistry that went into their production.

Historical Context

The **half cent** was first introduced in the United States in 1793, a time when the nation was still finding its footing. The coin was minted to facilitate commerce, particularly for smaller transactions. The **cent** followed closely behind, with its initial release in the same year. Both coins have undergone numerous design changes, reflecting shifts in artistic style and public sentiment.

Design Variations

Understanding the various **designs** of half cents and cents is crucial for collectors. The early half cents featured images of Liberty, while later versions showcased more intricate designs, such as the iconic Draped Bust and the Classic Head. Similarly, cents have transitioned from the **large cent** to the small cent, with the introduction of the famous Lincoln penny in 1909 marking a significant milestone. Each design tells a story, and knowing these narratives enhances the value of a collection.

Grading and Condition

Grading is an essential aspect of collecting half cents and cents. Coins are evaluated based on their **condition**, which can significantly impact their market value. Familiarizing yourself with grading scales, such as the Sheldon scale, will help you assess your coins accurately. Remember that even slight imperfections can shift a coin's grade, so always handle your collection with care.

Market Trends

The market for half cents and cents has seen various fluctuations over the years. Collectors should stay informed about current trends, including which coins are gaining popularity and which are declining in value. Factors such as **rarity**, historical significance, and condition play a crucial role in determining a coin's market worth. Engaging with fellow collectors and participating in forums can provide valuable insights into these trends.

Authentication Techniques

Authenticating coins is a critical concern for collectors, particularly with the prevalence of counterfeits. Familiarize yourself with **authentication techniques** and tools, such as magnifying glasses and digital calipers. Additionally, consider utilizing professional grading services for high-value coins. These services not only verify authenticity but also provide a reliable grade that can enhance your collection's credibility.

Building a Legacy

Many collectors view their collections as a way to create a **lasting legacy**. Half cents and cents can serve as a means to share history and knowledge with future generations. Consider involving your family in the collecting process. Teaching your children about the significance of these coins can foster a shared appreciation for history and craftsmanship.

Resources and Community Engagement

Engaging with the numismatic community can greatly enhance your collecting experience. Seek out local coin shows, clubs, and online forums where you can connect with other collectors. These interactions can provide valuable networking opportunities and insights into the latest market trends and collecting strategies.

Half cents and cents offer a fascinating glimpse into the past, serving both as a hobby and a potential investment. By understanding their history, design variations, grading, and authentication methods, you can build a collection that not only reflects your personal interests but also stands the test of time. Remember, the journey of collecting is as rewarding as the coins themselves, so embrace the process and enjoy every moment.

Nickels and Dimes

Nickels and dimes hold a unique place in the hearts of collectors, often serving as the gateway to the world of numismatics. These coins are not only practical in everyday transactions but also rich in history and variety. Understanding their significance can enhance your collecting experience and provide a solid foundation for building a meaningful collection.

Historical Context

The nickel, introduced in 1866, was initially created to replace the silver three-cent piece. Its composition has changed over the years, transitioning from a mix of silver and copper to the more common copper-nickel alloy we see today. The dime, on the other hand, has been in circulation since the late 18th century, with its design evolving through various artistic influences. Collectors often find joy in tracing the evolution of these coins, as each era tells a different story about the nation's economy and culture.

Types of Nickels

Among the various types of nickels, the **Buffalo nickel** and the **Jefferson nickel** stand out as favorites. The Buffalo nickel, minted from 1913 to 1938, features a Native American on one side and a buffalo on the other, symbolizing the American frontier. The Jefferson nickel, introduced in 1938, has undergone several design changes, including the introduction of the **Westward Journey Nickel Series** in 2004, which celebrated the Louisiana Purchase. Each type offers unique collecting opportunities, from mint marks to error coins.

Types of Dimes

Dimes also offer a rich variety for collectors. The **Mercury dime**, minted from 1916 to 1945, is particularly popular due to its beautiful design, which features a winged Liberty head. The **Roosevelt dime**, introduced in 1946, honors President Franklin D. Roosevelt and is notable for its role in fundraising for polio research. Collectors often seek out special editions, such as the **silver dimes** minted before 1965, which hold intrinsic value beyond their face value.

Grading and Condition

When it comes to nickels and dimes, understanding **grading** is essential for collectors. The condition of a coin significantly affects its value. Familiarizing yourself with the **Sheldon Scale**, which ranges from Poor (P-1) to Perfect Uncirculated (MS-70), can help you assess your coins accurately. Pay close attention to signs of wear, such as scratches or discoloration, which can drastically reduce a coin's market value.

Authentication Techniques

With the rise of counterfeit coins, knowing how to authenticate your nickels and dimes is crucial. Techniques such as **magnification** to inspect details, using a **scale** to check weight, and performing a **ping test** can help you determine a coin's authenticity. For those who are uncertain, seeking the assistance of a professional grading service can provide peace of mind and protect your investment.

Building Your Collection

When starting your collection, consider focusing on a specific theme, such as **type coins**, **mint marks**, or **historical periods**. This approach can make your collecting journey more enjoyable and targeted. Additionally, attending local coin shows and joining numismatic clubs can provide valuable resources and connections to fellow collectors who share your interests.

Investment Potential

Both nickels and dimes can serve as viable investment options. While they may not appreciate as rapidly as some other collectibles, their historical significance and rarity can lead to long-term value. Researching market trends and understanding the demand for specific coins can help you make informed decisions about your collection. Always remember, investing in coins should be a balance between passion and financial strategy.

Passing on the Legacy

One of the most rewarding aspects of coin collecting is the opportunity to share your passion with family. Consider involving your children in your collecting journey by teaching them about the historical significance of the coins and the stories behind them. This can foster a sense of appreciation for history and create lasting memories as you build a collection that may one day be passed down through generations.

Nickels and dimes are more than just currency; they are a window into our past and a means of connecting with future generations. By understanding their history, learning to authenticate and grade them, and engaging with the community, you can enhance your collecting experience. Remember, the journey of collecting is as valuable as the coins themselves, offering insights and stories that enrich your life.

Quarters and Half Dollars

When it comes to numismatics, **quarters and half dollars** hold a special place in the hearts of collectors. These coins not only represent a significant portion of American currency history but also offer a rich variety of designs and minting errors that can enhance any collection. Understanding the nuances of these coins is crucial for both novice and seasoned collectors alike.

Historical Significance

The history of quarters and half dollars is intertwined with the evolution of the United States itself. The **quarter** was first introduced in 1796, and over the years, it has undergone numerous design changes, reflecting the nation's values and milestones. Similarly, the **half dollar** has been a staple since 1794, serving as a symbol of economic stability. Collectors often seek specific dates and mint marks that can add historical context to their collections.

Popular Series to Collect

Among the most sought-after series are the **Washington quarters** and the **Kennedy half dollars**. The Washington quarter, which debuted in 1932, has seen various commemorative issues, including the popular **State Quarters** program launched in 1999. Meanwhile, the Kennedy half dollar, introduced in 1964 following the assassination of President John F. Kennedy, is known for its **silver content** and has a dedicated following among collectors.

Identifying Authenticity

One of the primary concerns for collectors is ensuring the authenticity of their coins. With the rise of counterfeiting, it's essential to know how to spot a fake. Look for **key details** such as the weight, dimensions, and mint marks. Utilizing a **magnifying glass** can help reveal subtle differences in design and lettering. Additionally, consider investing in a digital scale and caliper for precise measurements.

Investment Potential

Quarters and half dollars can also serve as viable investments. Certain coins, especially those with low mintage or unique errors, can appreciate significantly over time. For example, the **1964 Kennedy half dollar** is particularly valuable due to its silver content. Collectors should stay informed about market trends and consult resources like price guides to assess the value of their collections.

Engaging the Family

One of the joys of coin collecting is the opportunity to share your passion with family. Involving children in the hobby can create lasting memories and foster a sense of appreciation for history. Consider organizing family coin hunts or discussions about the stories behind specific coins. This not only enriches their understanding but also strengthens family bonds through shared experiences.

Community and Resources

Engaging with fellow collectors can enhance your knowledge and enjoyment of the hobby. Local coin clubs, online forums, and social media groups offer platforms to connect with others who share your interests. These communities can provide valuable insights into **authentication techniques**, market trends, and upcoming shows where you can buy, sell, or trade coins.

Dollars and Commemorative Coins

When it comes to coin collecting, **dollars and commemorative coins** hold a special place in the hearts of collectors. These coins not only represent significant monetary values but also capture historical moments and cultural milestones. Understanding the nuances of these coins can enhance your collection and provide a rich narrative to share with future generations.

Dollars have a long-standing history in the United States, evolving from the Spanish dollar to the modern coins we see today. The **Morgan dollar**, minted from 1878 to 1904 and again in 1921, is particularly sought after for its striking design and historical significance. Collectors often seek out specific mint marks or rare dates, which can dramatically increase a coin's value. When considering purchasing a Morgan dollar, pay attention to the coin's condition, as grading can significantly affect its market worth.

Another iconic dollar is the **Peace dollar**, introduced in 1921 to commemorate the end of World War I. The design, featuring Lady Liberty on the obverse and a majestic eagle on the reverse, symbolizes peace and hope. Collectors often look for coins with high mintages, but the rarer varieties can fetch substantial prices. Understanding the market trends and historical context behind these coins can help you make informed decisions while building your collection.

Moving on to **commemorative coins**, these pieces are often minted to honor specific events, individuals, or milestones. They are typically produced in limited quantities, making them attractive to collectors. For instance, the **Bicentennial commemorative coins**, issued in 1976, celebrated the 200th anniversary of the United States. These coins, featuring a unique design, often hold sentimental value for those who appreciate American history.

When collecting commemorative coins, it's essential to consider their **mintage numbers** and the significance of the event they represent. Limited editions often appreciate in value over time, especially if they are kept in pristine condition. Additionally, the inclusion of unique features, such as special finishes or designs, can also enhance a coin's desirability.

As you delve into the world of dollars and commemorative coins, be mindful of **authentication**. The market is rife with counterfeits, and ensuring that your coins are genuine is paramount. Familiarize yourself with the characteristics of authentic coins, such as weight, dimensions, and design details. Utilizing a reputable grading service can also provide peace of mind, especially for high-value purchases.

Another aspect to consider is the **historical context** surrounding your coins. Each piece tells a story, whether it's about the era it was minted in or the event it commemorates. Connecting with fellow collectors can provide insights and anecdotes that enrich your understanding and appreciation of your collection. Engaging with local coin clubs or online forums can facilitate discussions and connections that deepen your knowledge.

Lastly, as you build your collection of dollars and commemorative coins, think about the legacy you wish to create. Sharing your passion with family can foster a shared interest in numismatics. Consider involving your children in the collection process, teaching them about the history and significance of each coin. This engagement can create lasting memories and ensure that your love for coin collecting is passed down through generations.

In summary, dollars and commemorative coins are not just currency; they are tangible pieces of history. By understanding their significance, ensuring their authenticity, and sharing your passion with loved ones, you can create a collection that stands the test of time. Embrace the journey of collecting, and let each coin serve as a reminder of the stories and legacies they carry.

Gold Coins and Bullion

Gold coins have long been a symbol of wealth and prosperity, making them a popular choice among collectors and investors alike. Their intrinsic value, derived from the precious metal itself, often leads to appreciation over time. When it comes to gold coins, understanding their significance, types, and market dynamics is crucial for anyone looking to build a collection or invest wisely.

Types of Gold Coins

Gold coins come in various forms, each with its unique characteristics and appeal. The most common types include:

- **Investment Coins:** These are produced primarily for investment purposes and include well-known examples like the American Gold Eagle and the Canadian Gold Maple Leaf. They are typically minted with a specific weight and purity, making them easy to value.

- **Numismatic Coins:** These coins are collected for their historical significance, rarity, or aesthetic appeal rather than their gold content. Examples include ancient coins and limited-edition releases from various mints.

- **Gold Bullion Coins:** These coins are made from gold bullion and are valued based on their metal content. They often carry a premium over the spot price of gold, which can fluctuate based on market conditions.

Understanding Gold Coin Value

The value of gold coins is influenced by several factors, including:

- **Gold Spot Price:** The current market price for gold significantly impacts the value of gold coins. It's essential to stay updated on market trends to make informed purchasing decisions.

- **Coin Condition:** The condition of a coin, often graded on a scale from one to seventy, affects its desirability and value. Higher-grade coins typically command a premium.

- **Rarity:** Coins that are rare or have limited mintage can be more valuable than those that are widely available. Collectors often seek these unique pieces to enhance their collections.

Buying Gold Coins

When purchasing gold coins, it's vital to consider a few key points to avoid potential pitfalls:

- **Reputable Dealers:** Always buy from established and reputable dealers. Check for reviews and credentials to ensure you are dealing with a trustworthy source.

- **Authentication:** Be vigilant about verifying the authenticity of the coins. Look for certificates of authenticity or consider using professional grading services.

- **Price Comparison:** Compare prices from multiple dealers to ensure you are getting a fair deal. Prices can vary significantly, so it pays to shop around.

Storing Gold Coins

Proper storage is essential to protect your investment. Here are some tips:

- **Safe Storage:** Invest in a safe or safety deposit box to keep your coins secure. Avoid storing them in easily accessible places.

- **Handling:** Always handle coins with care. Use gloves to prevent oils from your skin from damaging the surface.

- **Insurance:** Consider insuring your collection. This can provide peace of mind in case of theft or damage.

Gold Coins as an Investment

Investing in gold coins can be a wise decision, especially during economic uncertainty. Gold often acts as a hedge against inflation and currency fluctuations. However, it's important to approach this investment with caution:

- **Diversification:** Don't put all your investment capital into gold coins. Diversifying your portfolio can help mitigate risks.

- **Market Research:** Stay informed about market trends and economic indicators that can affect gold prices.

- **Long-Term Perspective:** While gold can provide short-term gains, it is often viewed as a long-term investment. Be prepared to hold onto your coins for several years to realize their full potential.

Building a Legacy

As you embark on your journey in gold coin collecting, consider the legacy you wish to create. Passing down a collection to your children can be a fulfilling experience, allowing them to appreciate the history and value of your coins. Share your knowledge and passion with them, fostering an interest in numismatics that can last for generations.

In conclusion, gold coins offer both a fascinating hobby and a solid investment opportunity. By understanding the types of coins available, their value, and best practices for buying and storing them, you can navigate the world of gold collecting with confidence. Remember to approach your collection with a blend of passion and prudence, ensuring that your investment not only grows in value but also becomes a cherished part of your family's heritage.

Book 6: Specialty Coins and Advanced Collecting

Specialty coins represent a fascinating niche within the world of numismatics, appealing to collectors who seek unique pieces that tell a story or reflect a particular theme. Whether you're drawn to commemorative coins, error coins, or those with historical significance, understanding the nuances of these specialty areas can enhance your collecting experience and investment potential.

Commemorative Coins

Commemorative coins are issued to honor significant events, people, or milestones. These coins often feature intricate designs and limited mintage, making them particularly appealing to collectors. When considering commemorative coins, it's essential to research the **history behind each piece** and its significance. Some well-known examples include the **American Silver Eagle** and the **U.S. Mint's commemorative series** celebrating national parks or historical figures.

Error Coins

Error coins are a thrilling category for collectors, as they are produced due to mistakes during the minting process. These coins can range from minor discrepancies, such as **off-center strikes**, to major errors like **double dies** or **wrong planchets**. Collectors often find great value in these pieces, as their rarity can lead to significant appreciation over time. Always verify the authenticity of error coins, as the market can attract forgeries.

Historical Coins

Coins that hold historical significance often carry a story that resonates with collectors. Coins from ancient civilizations, such as **Greek or Roman coins**, provide a glimpse into the past and can be highly sought after. When collecting historical coins, consider not only their age but also their **cultural context** and the events they represent. This aspect can add depth to your collection and provide engaging narratives to share with others.

Investment Considerations

Investing in specialty coins can be rewarding, but it requires a strategic approach. Understand the **market trends** and demand for specific types of specialty coins. For instance, limited edition commemoratives may appreciate faster than more common coins. Additionally, consider the **condition and grading** of the coins, as these factors significantly impact value. Always seek reliable resources or expert opinions before making significant investments.

Resources for Collectors

Engaging with the numismatic community can enhance your collecting journey. Look for local coin shows, clubs, and online forums where you can connect with fellow enthusiasts. These platforms provide opportunities to **share knowledge**, trade coins, and gain insights from experienced collectors. Participating in discussions can also help you stay informed about the latest trends and developments in the specialty coin market.

Preserving Your Collection

Proper care and preservation of specialty coins are crucial for maintaining their value. Store your coins in **acid-free holders** or protective cases to prevent damage from environmental factors. Avoid handling coins directly; instead, use cotton gloves to minimize the risk of fingerprints and oils. Regularly check your collection for signs of wear or deterioration, and seek professional conservation services if necessary.

Passing Down Your Collection

As you build your specialty coin collection, consider the legacy you wish to leave. Involving your children or family members in the hobby can create lasting memories and foster a shared appreciation for numismatics. Share stories about each coin's significance and the lessons you've learned along the way. This engagement not only enriches their understanding but also ensures that your passion for coin collecting continues through future generations.

Final Thoughts

Specialty coins offer a unique avenue for collectors to explore their interests and invest in pieces that resonate with them. By focusing on authenticity, understanding market trends, and engaging with the community, you can navigate this exciting field with confidence. Remember, each coin has a story to tell—make sure yours is one worth sharing.

8. Specialty Coins and Series

Coin collecting is an art that transcends mere hobbyism; it is a journey into history, culture, and sometimes, investment. Among the myriad of options available, specialty coins and series stand out as particularly captivating avenues for collectors. These coins often tell unique stories, embody specific themes, or celebrate significant events, making them not just collectibles but also pieces of art and history.

Understanding Specialty Coins is fundamental for any collector looking to deepen their engagement with numismatics. Unlike standard coins, specialty coins often come with a narrative that enhances their value. For example, coins commemorating anniversaries of significant events or those that celebrate cultural milestones can draw collectors not only for their monetary worth but also for their historical significance. This dual appeal makes them a popular choice for both novice and seasoned collectors.

When diving into specialty coins, it's essential to consider **the themes that resonate with you**. Some collectors may be drawn to coins that represent their heritage, while others might find joy in collecting coins that honor specific historical figures or events. For instance, the American Silver Eagle series is not only popular for its silver content but also for its representation of American ideals. Understanding what themes resonate with you can guide your collection and make it more personally meaningful.

Popular Series provide a rich landscape for collectors. The state quarters program, for instance, introduced collectors to the beauty of regional diversity in the United States. Each quarter features a unique design that reflects the history or culture of the state it represents. Similarly, the Presidential dollar series offers a glimpse into the nation's leadership, showcasing the likenesses of past presidents. These series often have a built-in community of collectors who share insights, trade coins, and celebrate the stories behind each piece.

Another fascinating aspect of specialty coins is their **limited editions and proofs**. Many mints produce coins in limited quantities, which can significantly enhance their value over time. Proof coins, with their polished finish, are particularly sought after for their aesthetic appeal. Collectors should pay attention to the minting year, the production numbers, and the condition of the coins, as these factors play a crucial role in determining value. The thrill of acquiring a limited-edition piece can be exhilarating, but it's essential to conduct thorough research to ensure authenticity.

Authentication and Grading are paramount when dealing with specialty coins. The fear of counterfeits is a common concern among collectors, especially when purchasing high-value items. Familiarizing yourself with grading scales and authentication methods can empower you to make informed decisions. Seek out reputable dealers and consider using third-party grading services to ensure the coins in your collection meet the highest standards. This diligence not only protects your investment but also enhances your reputation within the collector community.

Engaging with **fellow collectors** can also enrich your experience with specialty coins. Whether through local coin shows, online forums, or numismatic clubs, sharing your passion with others can lead to valuable insights and opportunities. Networking with other collectors allows you to exchange knowledge, trade coins, and even collaborate on research projects. This sense of community can be particularly rewarding, as it fosters a shared appreciation for the history and artistry of coin collecting.

As you build your collection, consider how you might **pass on your passion** to future generations. Specialty coins can serve as wonderful heirlooms, each with its own story to tell. Engaging your family in the hobby not only strengthens familial bonds but also creates lasting memories. Share the stories behind your coins, teach them about the historical context, and involve them in the collecting process. This can instill a sense of pride and responsibility in your children, ensuring that your legacy continues.

In conclusion, specialty coins and series offer a rich tapestry of opportunities for collectors. By focusing on themes that resonate personally, engaging with fellow collectors, and prioritizing authentication, you can build a collection that is not only valuable but also deeply meaningful. Remember, each coin is a portal to the past, waiting for you to explore its story and share it with the world.

Error Coins and Varieties

When diving into the fascinating world of coin collecting, one of the most exciting aspects is discovering **error coins** and **varieties**. These unique pieces not only hold a special place in the hearts of collectors but also often carry significant value. Understanding what constitutes an error coin versus a variety is essential for any serious collector.

Error coins are those that have been produced with mistakes during the minting process. These errors can occur at any stage of production, leading to coins that deviate from the intended design or specifications. Common types of errors include **double strikes**, where a coin is struck twice by the die, resulting in overlapping images; **off-center strikes**, where the coin is not properly aligned during minting; and **die breaks**, which can create unexpected features on the coin's surface. Each of these errors can dramatically affect the coin's appearance and value, making them highly sought after by collectors.

On the other hand, **varieties** refer to coins that differ from the standard issue due to changes in design or features made intentionally by the mint. These can include variations in the date, mintmark, or even slight alterations in the design elements. For instance, the **1909-S V.D.B. penny** is one of the most famous varieties, known for its distinctive designer initials on the reverse. Collectors often seek out these varieties for their uniqueness and potential for appreciation in value.

Identifying error coins and varieties requires a keen eye and a solid understanding of the specific coins in your collection. It's crucial to familiarize yourself with the **standard characteristics** of the coins you are interested in, including their design, dimensions, and minting details. This foundational knowledge will help you spot deviations that could indicate an error or a variety.

When examining a coin, take your time to inspect it closely. Look for **anomalies** in the design, such as irregular shapes, unusual textures, or unexpected markings. A magnifying glass can be an invaluable tool in this process, allowing you to see fine details that might otherwise go unnoticed. Additionally, consider consulting **reference books** or online resources dedicated to error coins and varieties. These guides can provide images and descriptions that will aid in your identification efforts.

Another important aspect of collecting error coins and varieties is understanding their **market value**. Not all errors or varieties are created equal; some can be worth a small fortune, while others may only fetch a modest price. Factors influencing a coin's value include its rarity, condition, and demand among collectors. Keeping up with market trends through reputable numismatic publications or forums can help you gauge the current value of specific coins.

As you build your collection, consider documenting your findings. Keeping a detailed log of the error coins and varieties you acquire, along with their characteristics and provenance, can enhance the value of your collection. This documentation not only serves as a personal record but can also be beneficial if you choose to sell or pass down your collection in the future.

Engaging with the numismatic community is another excellent way to deepen your understanding of error coins and varieties. Attend local coin shows, participate in online forums, and connect with other collectors. These interactions can provide insights and tips that you may not find in books or articles. Plus, sharing your experiences can lead to valuable discussions about the intricacies of error coins and varieties.

Ultimately, collecting error coins and varieties can be a rewarding and enriching experience. The thrill of discovering a rare piece or identifying an error can bring joy and satisfaction to your collecting journey. By honing your skills in identification, staying informed about market trends, and engaging with fellow collectors, you can build a collection that not only holds personal significance but also has the potential for lasting value.

As you continue to explore this captivating aspect of numismatics, remember that each error coin and variety tells a story—a story of the minting process, the hands it has passed through, and the collector's journey. Embrace the adventure, and let your passion for coin collecting flourish.

Proof and Mint Sets

Proof and mint sets are a fascinating aspect of coin collecting, appealing to both beginners and seasoned collectors alike. These sets not only showcase the artistry and craftsmanship of coin production but also hold significant value for collectors. Understanding the nuances of proof and mint sets can enhance your collection and investment strategy.

What Are Proof Sets? Proof sets are collections of coins that have been specially struck to produce a high-quality finish. The coins in these sets are made using a different process than standard coins, resulting in a mirror-like surface and sharper details. Typically, proof sets are issued by the U.S. Mint and include coins from a specific year, often showcasing designs that reflect that year's themes or commemorative events.

Characteristics of Proof Coins The most distinguishing feature of proof coins is their finish. They are struck multiple times using polished dies, which gives them a brilliant, reflective surface. This striking process also enhances the details, making proof coins visually stunning. Collectors often seek proof coins for their beauty and the technical excellence they represent.

Mint Sets Explained Mint sets, on the other hand, consist of coins that are produced for circulation but packaged together by the U.S. Mint. Unlike proof coins, mint set coins are not specially treated for a high finish. Instead, they are struck with standard production methods and are meant to represent the coins that were released for public use in a given year. Mint sets typically include one of each denomination produced by the mint during that year.

Why Collect Proof and Mint Sets? Collecting proof and mint sets can be an excellent way to diversify your numismatic portfolio. Proof sets often appreciate in value due to their limited production runs and the quality of the coins, making them a sound investment choice. Mint sets, while generally more affordable, can also appreciate over time, especially if they contain coins that are in high demand or have historical significance.

Investment Considerations When considering proof and mint sets as an investment, it's essential to research the market trends. Some years see higher demand for specific sets, while others may not hold as much value. Pay attention to the condition of the coins, as well-preserved sets will command higher prices. Additionally, the packaging and certificates of authenticity can play a significant role in a set's value, so always keep these elements intact.

Storage and Care Proper storage is crucial for maintaining the quality of your proof and mint sets. Use protective holders that prevent tarnishing and scratches, and store them in a cool, dry place away from direct sunlight. Handling coins with care is essential; always hold them by the edges to avoid fingerprints and oils from your skin affecting their surfaces.

Building a Collection To build a meaningful collection of proof and mint sets, consider focusing on specific themes or years that resonate with you. Some collectors choose to collect sets from particular decades, while others may focus on commemorative issues. Engaging with other collectors through forums or local coin shows can provide insights and tips for expanding your collection.

Community Engagement Joining a community of collectors can enhance your experience and knowledge in collecting proof and mint sets. Online forums and local clubs often host discussions about the latest trends, authentication techniques, and investment strategies. Sharing your passion and learning from others can help you navigate the complexities of numismatics.

Final Thoughts Proof and mint sets represent a unique intersection of art, history, and investment potential. Whether you're a novice collector or a seasoned numismatist, understanding the intricacies of these sets can enrich your collecting journey. As you build your collection, remember to focus on authenticity, proper care, and community engagement to maximize your enjoyment and investment success.

Tokens and Medals

Tokens and medals are fascinating components of numismatics that often capture the interest of collectors beyond traditional coins. These items, while distinct from standard currency, offer rich historical narratives and unique aesthetic qualities that can enhance any collection.

Understanding Tokens

Tokens are typically made of metal and were originally created for various purposes, such as trade, advertising, or as a means of payment in specific contexts. They can be found in a multitude of forms, from simple round pieces to intricately designed shapes. Collectors often seek tokens for their **historical significance** and the stories they tell about local economies, industries, and communities.

Types of Tokens

There are several categories of tokens, each with distinct characteristics. **Trade tokens** were often issued by businesses as a form of currency that could only be used within their establishments. **Transportation tokens** were used for public transit systems, while **event tokens** commemorated fairs or exhibitions. Understanding these categories can help collectors appreciate the context in which these tokens were used and their significance in numismatic history.

Medals: A Different Kind of Collectible

Medals, on the other hand, are typically struck or cast to commemorate a person, event, or achievement. Unlike tokens, medals are not meant for circulation as currency. They often feature intricate designs and inscriptions that reflect their commemorative purpose. Collectors value medals for their **artistic merit** and the historical events they represent.

Types of Medals

Medals can be categorized into various types, including **military medals**, awarded for service or valor, and **commemorative medals**, which celebrate significant events or milestones. **Society medals** are also popular, often awarded by organizations to recognize achievements or contributions. Each category offers a window into different facets of history and culture.

Collecting Considerations

When adding tokens and medals to your collection, consider their **condition**, **rarity**, and **provenance**. The condition of an item can significantly affect its value, so familiarize yourself with grading systems specific to tokens and medals. Rarity often drives demand, so seek out pieces that are less commonly found. Provenance, or the history of ownership, can also add value and interest to your items.

Authentication and Avoiding Scams

As with coins, the authenticity of tokens and medals is paramount. Be vigilant about **counterfeits**, especially with popular or high-value items. Learn to recognize signs of authenticity, such as weight, dimensions, and design details. Connecting with reputable dealers and attending numismatic shows can also provide opportunities to learn from experts and avoid potential pitfalls.

Displaying Your Collection

Once you've curated a collection of tokens and medals, consider how to display them. Proper **display techniques** not only protect your items but also enhance their visual appeal. Use display cases that prevent tarnishing and allow for easy viewing. Consider thematic arrangements that tell a story or highlight specific aspects of your collection.

Engaging with the Community

Engaging with other collectors can enrich your understanding and appreciation of tokens and medals. Look for local clubs, online forums, or social media groups where enthusiasts share insights, trade items, and discuss their experiences. These communities can be invaluable resources for learning and connecting with like-minded individuals.

Passing Down the Legacy

As you build your collection, think about how you can **involve your family** in this hobby. Sharing your passion for tokens and medals can create lasting memories and instill an appreciation for history and craftsmanship in the next generation. Consider hosting family discussions or even small workshops where you can teach them about the significance of your collection.

Bullion and Precious Metals

When it comes to **bullion and precious metals**, collectors often find themselves navigating a complex landscape of investment opportunities and market fluctuations. Understanding the fundamentals of bullion can not only enhance your collection but also provide a solid foundation for investment strategies.

The most commonly recognized forms of bullion include **gold, silver, platinum, and palladium**. Each of these metals has unique characteristics and market behaviors, making it essential for collectors to familiarize themselves with their properties before diving into purchases. For instance, gold has historically been viewed as a safe-haven asset, often retaining its value during economic downturns, while silver can be more volatile but is often used in industrial applications, impacting its market price.

Investing in bullion can be approached in several ways. Many collectors choose to buy **coins or bars** that are minted by government authorities or recognized private mints. Coins often carry a **numismatic value** beyond their metal content, especially if they are rare or in high demand. On the other hand, bullion bars typically offer a lower premium over the spot price of the metal, making them a more cost-effective option for bulk purchases.

When considering your investment, it's crucial to keep an eye on the **spot price** of the metals. This price fluctuates based on market conditions, so timing your purchase can significantly affect your overall investment return. Many online platforms and financial news outlets provide real-time updates on spot prices, which can aid in making informed buying decisions.

Storage and security are also critical aspects of bullion collecting. Whether you choose to keep your metals at home or in a secure vault, understanding the risks associated with theft and damage is essential. Many collectors opt for **safe deposit boxes** or specialized storage facilities that offer insurance and enhanced security measures.

Another important consideration is **liquidity**. The ease with which you can sell your bullion can greatly impact your investment strategy. Coins from well-known mints tend to be more liquid than generic bars, as they are widely recognized and sought after by collectors and investors alike. Familiarize yourself with reputable dealers and platforms where you can buy and sell bullion, ensuring you have options when it comes time to liquidate your assets.

As you delve deeper into the world of bullion, keep an eye out for **market trends** and economic indicators that can influence the prices of precious metals. Factors such as inflation rates, currency strength, and geopolitical events can all play a role in the market dynamics of bullion. Staying informed will enable you to make strategic decisions regarding your collection and investments.

Lastly, consider the **tax implications** of buying and selling bullion. Depending on your jurisdiction, there may be specific regulations regarding capital gains tax, which can affect your overall profit when selling your metals. Consulting with a financial advisor who understands the intricacies of precious metals investments can help you navigate these waters effectively.

In conclusion, bullion and precious metals can be a rewarding addition to your collection and investment portfolio. By understanding the characteristics of different metals, staying informed about market trends, and considering the practical aspects of storage and liquidity, you can build a collection that not only holds aesthetic value but also serves as a sound financial investment for the future.

Book 7: Valuation and Investment

Understanding the value of your coin collection is a crucial aspect of numismatics, especially for those who view their hobby as not only a passion but also a potential investment. The world of coin valuation can seem daunting, but breaking it down into manageable concepts can help you navigate this landscape with confidence.

Factors Influencing Coin Value

Several factors play a significant role in determining the value of a coin. These include:

- **Rarity:** The less common a coin is, the more valuable it typically becomes. Coins that were minted in limited quantities or that have been removed from circulation are often sought after.

- **Condition:** A coin's grade, which ranges from poor to perfect, significantly impacts its value. Coins that are well-preserved and exhibit minimal wear are generally worth more.

- **Demand:** The market demand for specific coins can fluctuate based on trends, collector interest, and historical significance. Keeping an eye on current market trends can provide insight into potential value increases.

- **Historical Significance:** Coins with interesting histories, such as those linked to significant events or figures, often command higher prices.

Methods of Valuation

Valuing your coins can be done through various methods, each with its own merits:

- **Price Guides:** Utilizing published price guides can give you a baseline for your coins' values. These guides are typically updated annually and reflect current market conditions.

- **Auction Results:** Studying auction results can provide real-world selling prices for similar coins. This method is particularly useful for understanding how much collectors are willing to pay.

- **Professional Appraisal:** For high-value coins or entire collections, hiring a professional appraiser can be beneficial. These experts can provide detailed insights and an accurate valuation based on their extensive knowledge and experience.

Investing in Coins

Investing in coins can be a rewarding venture, but it's essential to approach it with caution and knowledge. Here are some key considerations:

- **Long-Term Perspective:** Coin collecting should be viewed as a long-term investment. While some coins may appreciate quickly, many require time to increase in value significantly.

- **Diversification:** Just as with any investment portfolio, diversifying your coin collection can mitigate risk. Consider investing in different types of coins, such as bullion, numismatic, and historical pieces.

- **Education:** Continuously educating yourself about coin values, market trends, and collecting strategies is vital. Join forums, read books, and attend shows to enhance your knowledge.

Common Mistakes to Avoid

As you navigate the world of coin valuation and investment, be wary of common pitfalls:

- **Overpaying:** It's easy to get caught up in the excitement of a purchase. Always do your research and ensure you're paying a fair price based on the coin's value.

- **Ignoring Market Trends:** The coin market can be volatile. Ignoring shifts in demand or changes in collector interest can lead to poor investment decisions.

- **Neglecting Authentication:** Before investing in a valuable coin, ensure it's authentic. Counterfeit coins can severely diminish the value of your collection.

Building a Legacy

For many collectors, the goal extends beyond personal enjoyment to creating a legacy that can be shared with future generations. Here are some tips to consider:

- **Documentation:** Keep detailed records of your collection, including purchase prices, appraisals, and any historical information about the coins. This documentation will be invaluable for your heirs.

- **Involve Family:** Engage your family in your collecting journey. Share your knowledge and passion for coins, fostering an appreciation that may inspire them to continue the legacy.

- **Plan for Transfer:** Consider how you will pass on your collection. Whether through gifting, selling, or creating a trust, having a plan ensures your collection remains cherished. Valuation and investment in coin collecting require a thoughtful approach. By understanding the factors that influence value, employing effective valuation methods, and avoiding common mistakes, you can build a collection that not only brings you joy but also serves as a valuable asset. Remember, the journey of collecting is as important as the coins themselves, and sharing this passion with your family can create lasting memories and a meaningful legacy.

9. Grading and Evaluating Coins

Grading coins is an essential skill for any collector, as it directly impacts the value and desirability of your collection. Understanding how to evaluate coins accurately can enhance your confidence in transactions and help you make informed decisions. The process of grading involves examining various aspects of a coin, including its surface, luster, and overall appearance.

Understanding the Grading Scale

The most widely accepted grading scale is the **Sheldon Scale**, which ranges from 1 to 70. A grade of 1 indicates a coin that is heavily worn and barely recognizable, while a grade of 70 represents a coin in perfect condition. Familiarizing yourself with this scale is crucial, as it provides a common language for discussing coin quality.

Key Factors in Grading

When grading a coin, several factors come into play:

- **Wear and Tear:** Look for signs of wear, such as flat spots on high points and loss of detail.

- **Luster:** Observe how light interacts with the surface. A coin with original luster will appear bright and shiny.

- **Surface Quality:** Check for scratches, nicks, or blemishes that can detract from a coin's value.

- **Strike Quality:** Evaluate the sharpness of the design. A well-struck coin will have clear details and defined edges.

- **Color:** Note any unusual coloration, which may indicate cleaning or other damage.

Visual Aids for Grading

Utilizing **visual aids** can significantly enhance your grading skills. High-quality images of coins at different grades can serve as a valuable reference. Consider creating a grading guide with images that showcase various grades side by side, allowing you to compare coins directly.

Practice Makes Perfect

Grading coins is a skill that improves with practice. Start by examining coins from your collection or local shows. **Take notes** on your observations and compare them with established grades. Over time, you'll develop a keener eye for details and nuances that impact a coin's grade.

Common Grading Mistakes

Even experienced collectors can make mistakes when grading coins. Here are some common pitfalls to avoid:

- **Overgrading:** It's tempting to assign a higher grade than a coin deserves, especially if you have an emotional attachment to it.

- **Ignoring the Basics:** Always start with the fundamental aspects of grading before diving into finer details.

- **Relying Solely on Tools:** While magnification tools are helpful, they should not replace your overall assessment of the coin.

Seeking Professional Help

If you're ever uncertain about a coin's grade, consider seeking help from a **professional grader**. Many reputable grading services offer evaluations and can provide an unbiased assessment of your coins. This can be especially valuable for high-value pieces or when you're preparing to sell or trade.

Engaging with the Community

Participating in local coin clubs or online forums can also enhance your grading skills. Sharing your experiences and learning from others can provide insights that you may not have considered. Many collectors are more than willing to share their knowledge and help newcomers navigate the grading process.

Building Your Confidence

As you gain experience in grading, your confidence will grow. Remember that every collector has their unique perspective, and grading can sometimes be subjective. Trust your instincts, but always be open to learning and refining your skills.

Documenting Your Grading Process

Keeping a grading journal can be an excellent way to track your progress and document your findings. Write down the details of each coin you evaluate, including the grade you assigned and the reasons behind your decision. This practice not only reinforces your learning but also serves as a valuable reference for future evaluations.Grading and evaluating coins is a rewarding aspect of numismatics that can enhance your collecting experience. By understanding the grading scale, practicing regularly, and engaging with the community, you'll develop the skills necessary to assess coins accurately.

The Basics of Coin Grading

When it comes to coin collecting, understanding the basics of coin grading is essential. Grading is the process of assessing the condition of a coin, which significantly influences its value. Whether you're a beginner or have been collecting for years, having a solid grasp of grading principles can help you make informed decisions about buying, selling, or trading coins.

Coin grading is primarily categorized into two systems: the **numerical grading scale** and the **adjectival grading scale**. The numerical scale ranges from 1 to 70, with 70 representing a perfect coin. Coins graded 60 or above are generally considered to be in uncirculated condition. On the other hand, the adjectival scale uses terms like "Good," "Fine," "Very Fine," and "Uncirculated" to describe a coin's condition. Understanding these scales will help you communicate effectively with other collectors and dealers.

One of the most critical aspects of grading is recognizing the **key elements** that indicate a coin's condition. These elements include wear, luster, strike quality, and surface preservation. Wear refers to the loss of detail due to circulation, while luster indicates the coin's shine and reflects its freshness. The strike quality is determined by how well the coin was minted, and surface preservation looks at any marks or blemishes that may affect the coin's overall appeal.When evaluating a coin, it's essential to take a close look at both the **obverse** (front) and **reverse** (back) sides. Examine the design details, inscriptions, and any unique features that may set the coin apart. For example, if you're looking at a rare coin, even minor imperfections can significantly impact its value. Thus, paying attention to detail is crucial.

Another important factor is the **coin's history**. Coins that have been well-documented, especially those with interesting stories or provenance, often carry a higher value. Collectors are not just interested in the coin itself; they also appreciate the history behind it. This aspect can also be a great conversation starter at coin shows, helping you build connections within the community.To aid in the grading process, consider using a **magnifying glass** or a jeweler's loupe. These tools allow you to examine the coin closely, revealing details that may not be visible to the naked eye. Additionally, investing in a good grading guide or reference book can provide valuable insights into the grading process and help you become more confident in your evaluations.

When it comes to grading coins, it's also essential to recognize the potential for **subjectivity**. Different graders may have varying opinions on a coin's condition. This variability is why it's crucial to familiarize yourself with the grading standards used by reputable organizations, such as the **Professional Coin Grading Service (PCGS)** or the **Numismatic Guaranty Corporation (NGC)**. These organizations provide consistent grading guidelines that can help you assess your coins more accurately.

Professional Grading Services

When it comes to coin collecting, the role of **professional grading services** cannot be overstated. These organizations provide an essential function in the numismatic community by offering an unbiased assessment of a coin's quality and authenticity. By understanding how these services operate and their significance, collectors can make more informed decisions about their investments.

Professional grading services evaluate coins based on a standardized grading scale, which ranges from **Poor (P-1)** to **Perfect (MS-70)**. This grading system helps collectors gauge the condition of their coins accurately. For instance, a coin graded as **MS-65** is considered to be in excellent condition with minimal imperfections, while a coin graded as **AU-50** shows noticeable wear. Understanding these grades allows collectors to assess the potential value of their coins more effectively.

One of the primary benefits of utilizing a professional grading service is the assurance of **authenticity**. Counterfeit coins are a significant concern in the collecting world, and having a coin graded by a reputable service can provide peace of mind. These organizations employ experts who use advanced technology and extensive knowledge to determine whether a coin is genuine. This authentication process protects collectors from the risk of purchasing fakes, which can lead to financial losses and embarrassment among peers.

Additionally, coins that are graded by professional services often command higher prices in the market. Collectors are generally willing to pay a premium for coins that come with a grading certificate, as it adds a layer of trust and credibility to the transaction. This is particularly important for those looking to build a collection that will stand the test of time and be passed down to future generations. A well-documented collection, complete with grading certificates, can significantly enhance its value.

When selecting a grading service, it's essential to consider the reputation and reliability of the organization. Well-known grading companies, such as the **Professional Coin Grading Service (PCGS)** and the **Numismatic Guaranty Corporation (NGC)**, have established themselves as leaders in the field. These organizations have rigorous standards and are recognized globally, making them trustworthy options for collectors. Researching reviews and testimonials can also provide insight into the experiences of other collectors with specific grading services.

Another factor to consider is the **turnaround time** for grading submissions. Depending on the service, the time it takes to receive a graded coin can vary significantly. Some companies offer expedited services for an additional fee, which can be beneficial for collectors eager to know the grade of their coins quickly. However, it's crucial to weigh the cost against the potential benefits, especially if the coin is not of high value.

In addition to grading, many professional services offer **additional resources** that can enhance a collector's experience. This may include access to market trends, price guides, and educational materials. These resources can be invaluable for both novice and experienced collectors, as they provide insights that can aid in making informed purchasing decisions. Engaging with these resources can also help collectors stay updated on the latest developments in the numismatic world.

It's also worth noting that not all coins require professional grading. For some collectors, particularly those just starting, it may be more practical to focus on building a collection through personal research and learning about grading basics. However, as a collection grows and the value of individual coins increases, seeking professional grading services becomes more critical.

In conclusion, professional grading services play a vital role in the coin collecting community. They provide essential authentication, enhance the value of coins, and offer a wealth of resources for collectors. By understanding the importance of these services and selecting a reputable organization, collectors can navigate the complexities of the numismatic world with greater confidence and assurance.

Evaluating Condition and Rarity

When it comes to evaluating the condition and rarity of coins, it's essential to understand that both factors play a crucial role in determining a coin's overall value. Collectors need to be equipped with the right knowledge to make informed decisions, whether they're purchasing coins or assessing the ones they already own.

Understanding Coin Grades

Coin grading is the process of assessing a coin's condition on a scale, typically from 1 to 70. The higher the grade, the better the condition. Here's a brief overview of the grading scale:

- **Good (G) Coins that are heavily worn with details barely visible. They are often considered the lowest collectible grade.**

- **Fine (F)**: Coins that show clear details but have noticeable wear. They are more appealing than Good coins.

- **Very Fine (VF)**: Coins with moderate wear, where most details are still visible. They are a step up from Fine coins.

- **Extremely Fine (EF)**: Coins that show only slight wear. They are close to uncirculated condition.

- **About Uncirculated (AU)**: Coins that have minimal wear, with most details intact. They are highly sought after.

- **Mint State (MS)**: Coins that have never been circulated and show no signs of wear. They are considered the best condition.

- **Proof (PR)**: Coins that are specially minted for collectors, often with a mirror-like finish.

Factors Affecting Coin Condition

Several factors can influence a coin's condition, and understanding these can help collectors make better evaluations:

- **Wear and Tear**: The more a coin has been handled, the more wear it will show. Look for scratches, dents, and other imperfections.

- **Cleaning**: Coins that have been cleaned can lose their value significantly. Always check for signs of polishing or harsh cleaning methods.

- **Environmental Damage**: Exposure to moisture, air, and contaminants can lead to corrosion or tarnishing. Be vigilant about how coins are stored.

- **Originality**: Coins that have retained their original surfaces are more valuable than those that have been altered or tampered with.

Assessing Rarity

Rarity is another critical component in determining a coin's value. Not all coins are created equal, and some are much harder to find than others. Here are some key points to consider:

- **Mintages**: The number of coins produced in a given year can significantly impact rarity. Lower mintages often equate to higher value.

- **Survivor Rates**: Even if a coin had a high mintage, if few examples remain today due to loss or destruction, its rarity increases.

- **Demand**: A coin can be rare, but if there's little interest in it, its value may not reflect its rarity. Conversely, high demand for a rare coin can drive prices up.

- **Historical Significance**: Coins that have a rich history or are associated with significant events tend to be more sought after, enhancing their rarity.

Practical Tips for Evaluation

Now that we've covered the fundamentals of grading and rarity, here are some practical tips to help you evaluate your coins effectively:

- **Use a Magnifying Glass**: A good magnifying glass can help you spot minute details that affect grading, such as scratches or signs of cleaning.

- **Familiarize Yourself with Reference Materials**: Invest in a reliable coin grading guide or book. These resources provide images and descriptions that can aid in accurate evaluations.

- **Join a Coin Collecting Community**: Engaging with fellow collectors can provide valuable insights and feedback on your evaluations.

- **Seek Professional Grading Services**: For high-value coins, consider sending them to a professional grading service. This not only provides an official grade but can also enhance the coin's marketability.

Final Thoughts

Evaluating the condition and rarity of coins is an essential skill for any collector. By understanding grading scales, recognizing factors that affect condition, and being aware of what makes a coin rare, you can make informed decisions that enhance your collection's value. Remember, the journey of collecting is as much about the coins themselves as it is about the stories and legacies they carry. With this knowledge, you can confidently navigate the world of numismatics and build a collection that you can proudly share with future generations.

10. Understanding Coin Values

Understanding the value of coins is a critical aspect of becoming a successful collector. It's not just about the price tags; it's about the factors that contribute to a coin's worth and how you can leverage this knowledge to build a valuable collection.

The first step in grasping coin values is to recognize that they are determined by a combination of factors, including **rarity**, **condition**, **demand**, and **historical significance**. Each of these elements plays a vital role in establishing the market price of a coin.

Rarity

The **rarity** of a coin significantly impacts its value. Coins that were minted in limited quantities or those that were produced for a short period tend to be more valuable. For instance, a coin that was only struck for a single year or a specific mint is often sought after by collectors, driving up its price. Understanding mintage figures and the historical context behind a coin's production can help you identify which coins may be more valuable due to their rarity.

Condition

The **condition** of a coin is another crucial determinant of its value. Coins are graded on a scale that ranges from poor to perfect, with higher grades commanding higher prices. Familiarize yourself with the grading system, such as the Sheldon scale, which ranges from 1 (poor) to 70 (perfect). Observing the coin's surface, luster, and any wear or damage will help you assess its condition accurately. Remember, even slight imperfections can affect a coin's value significantly.

Demand

Demand plays a pivotal role in the coin market. Even rare coins can fluctuate in value based on current trends and collector interest. For example, if a particular series of coins gains popularity due to a new trend or an influential collector, their prices can soar. Stay informed about market trends through reputable numismatic publications and online forums to gauge what's currently in demand.

Historical Significance

The **historical significance** of a coin can also enhance its value. Coins that are linked to significant events, people, or periods in history often attract collectors who are interested in the story behind the coin. For instance, coins that commemorate major historical milestones or figures can command a premium due to their cultural importance. Understanding the history surrounding your coins can add depth to your collection and potentially increase its value.

Price Guides and Resources

Utilizing **price guides** and resources is essential for determining coin values accurately. There are various publications, both print and digital, that provide updated pricing information based on market trends. The **Red Book**, for example, is a well-respected resource among collectors, offering detailed information on various coins, including their estimated values. Additionally, online platforms like eBay can provide insight into real-time selling prices, helping you understand what collectors are willing to pay.

Professional Appraisals

For those looking to ensure accuracy, seeking a **professional appraisal** can be invaluable. Professional numismatists can provide detailed assessments of your coins, often including documentation that can help establish provenance and value. This is particularly important if you are considering selling or insuring your collection. Knowing that your coins have been appraised by an expert can also give you peace of mind regarding their value.

Market Fluctuations

It's essential to recognize that the coin market can be volatile. Prices can change based on economic conditions, collector sentiment, and even changes in the supply of certain coins. Staying informed about the market and being adaptable will help you make better decisions regarding buying and selling coins. Regularly checking market trends and being part of collector communities can provide valuable insights.

Building Your Collection

When building your collection, focus on **quality over quantity**. A few high-quality coins can often be more valuable than a large number of lower-quality pieces. As you acquire coins, consider their potential for appreciation in value over time. Investing in coins that have strong historical significance, rarity, and demand is a strategic approach that can pay off in the long run.

Understanding coin values is not just about knowing how much a coin is worth; it's about appreciating the factors that contribute to its value. By focusing on rarity, condition, demand, and historical significance, and by utilizing resources and professional appraisals, you can make informed decisions that will enhance your collecting experience. Remember, the journey of coin collecting is as much about the stories and history behind the coins as it is about their monetary value, and sharing this passion with your family can create lasting memories that transcend generations.

Market Dynamics

The world of coin collecting is influenced by a variety of market dynamics that can significantly affect both the value of coins and the strategies collectors use. Understanding these dynamics is crucial for anyone looking to build a successful collection or make informed investments.

Supply and Demand

At the heart of any market is the principle of **supply and demand**. When demand for a particular coin increases, its value typically rises, especially if the supply is limited. For instance, rare coins or those with historical significance often see a spike in interest during anniversaries or public events. Collectors should keep an eye on trends and be aware that market fluctuations can occur based on various factors, including economic conditions and cultural shifts.

Market Trends

Staying informed about current **market trends** is essential for collectors. This includes understanding which coins are gaining popularity and which are falling out of favor. For example, certain types of coins may see increased demand due to media coverage, celebrity endorsements, or even social media trends. Regularly checking numismatic publications, attending shows, and participating in online forums can provide valuable insights into these trends.

Economic Factors

The broader economic climate can also have a profound impact on the coin market. During times of economic uncertainty, collectors may turn to tangible assets like coins as a form of **investment** and security. Conversely, when the economy is booming, collectors may feel more confident spending on higher-value items. Understanding these economic indicators can help collectors make more informed decisions about when to buy or sell.

Authentication and Grading

As mentioned earlier, the authenticity and grading of coins are pivotal in determining their market value. The presence of reputable grading services and authentication processes can enhance confidence among buyers. Collectors should familiarize themselves with the grading scale and seek out coins that have been certified by recognized authorities. This not only protects against counterfeits but also adds value to the collection.

Collector Demographics

The demographics of collectors can influence market dynamics as well. For example, younger collectors may prefer modern coins and collectibles that resonate with their interests, while older collectors might focus on historical pieces. Understanding these demographic shifts can help collectors anticipate changes in market demand and adjust their collecting strategies accordingly.

Global Influence

The coin market is not limited to local or national boundaries; it is a **global marketplace**. Economic conditions, cultural interests, and trends in other countries can significantly affect the North American market. Collectors should be aware of international trends and consider expanding their collecting horizons to include coins from around the world. This diversification can not only enhance their collection but also provide additional investment opportunities.

Scams and Fraud Prevention

As with any market, the coin collecting world is not without its share of **scams and fraud**. Collectors must remain vigilant, particularly when purchasing high-value items. Researching reputable dealers, utilizing authentication services, and staying informed about common scams can help protect against potential losses. Building a network of trustworthy contacts in the numismatic community can also provide valuable support and information.

Community Engagement

Engagement with the coin collecting community can greatly enhance a collector's experience. Participating in local clubs, attending shows, and joining online forums can provide opportunities for learning and networking. Sharing knowledge and experiences with fellow collectors can lead to valuable insights into market dynamics and investment strategies, ultimately enriching one's collecting journey.

Legacy and Family Involvement

Lastly, many collectors are motivated by the desire to create a **legacy** that can be passed down to future generations. Involving family members in the collecting process can foster a shared interest and ensure that the knowledge and passion for coin collecting are carried on. This familial connection not only enhances the enjoyment of the hobby but also helps to create lasting memories and traditions.

In conclusion, understanding the market dynamics of coin collecting is essential for anyone looking to navigate this fascinating hobby successfully. By staying informed about supply and demand, market trends, economic factors, and community engagement, collectors can make more informed decisions and enjoy a rewarding collecting experience.

Price Guides and Resources

When it comes to building your coin collection, understanding the value of your coins is crucial. Price guides are essential tools that can help you navigate the often murky waters of coin valuation. They provide a framework for assessing how much a coin is worth based on its rarity, condition, and market demand. **Investing in a reliable price guide** is one of the most effective ways to stay informed about your collection's worth. There are several types of price guides available, each serving different needs. **Printed guides**, such as the "Red Book" for U.S. coins, are popular among collectors. They offer comprehensive listings of coins along with historical context, grading standards, and price ranges.

However, printed guides can quickly become outdated, so it's wise to supplement them with **online resources**.

Online platforms like NumisMedia and CoinMarketCap provide real-time pricing data, allowing you to track fluctuations in the market. These resources often incorporate user-generated data, which can give you a more accurate picture of what collectors are willing to pay. While these platforms are invaluable, remember that prices can vary based on **condition** and **market trends**. Another important aspect of using price guides is understanding the difference between retail prices and wholesale prices. Retail prices are what you might expect to pay in a coin shop or online, while wholesale prices are what dealers might pay for coins in bulk. Knowing this distinction can help you negotiate better deals when buying or selling coins. As you delve deeper into the world of numismatics, consider joining local coin clubs or online forums. These communities can provide insights and recommendations on the best price guides to use. They can also help you stay updated on market trends and offer advice on how to assess the value of your coins more accurately. **Engaging with fellow collectors** can be an enriching experience, allowing you to learn from others' successes and mistakes. When utilizing price guides, always remember to cross-reference information. No single source will provide a definitive value for your coins. By comparing multiple guides and online resources, you can arrive at a more accurate estimation of your coin's worth. This practice also helps you avoid potential scams, as you'll have a broader understanding of what constitutes a fair price. In addition to price guides, consider investing in tools like **magnifying glasses** or **digital scales** to help assess the condition and authenticity of your coins. Understanding grading scales, such as the Sheldon Scale, is essential for determining a coin's value. A coin in excellent condition will command a higher price than one with visible wear and tear. **Learning how to grade coins** not only enhances your collecting experience but also empowers you to make informed purchasing decisions. Finally, keep in mind that the world of coin collecting is ever-evolving. Market values can shift due to various factors, including economic conditions and collector interest. Staying informed through ongoing education and engagement with the community will ensure that your coin collection remains a source of pride and potential investment for years to come. Always be prepared to adapt and learn; this flexibility will serve you well in your numismatic journey. In summary, utilizing price guides effectively requires a combination of reliable resources, community engagement, and a keen eye for detail. By arming yourself with knowledge and tools, you can navigate the complexities of coin valuation and build a collection that not only holds personal significance but also financial value.

Factors Affecting Coin Value

The world of coin collecting is fascinating, but understanding what affects **coin value** is crucial for both novice and seasoned collectors. Several factors come into play when determining how much a coin is worth, and being aware of these can help you make informed decisions, whether you're buying or selling.

Rarity is one of the most significant factors influencing a coin's value. The fewer coins that exist, the more valuable they tend to be. This rarity can stem from a limited mintage, coins that were never widely circulated, or those that were destroyed over time. Collectors often seek out rare coins to enhance their collections, and this demand can drive up prices considerably.

Condition also plays a pivotal role in determining value. Coins are graded on a scale, with higher grades indicating better condition. A coin in **mint condition** will fetch a higher price than one that is heavily worn or damaged. Understanding how to assess a coin's condition is essential for any collector, as it directly impacts its market value.

Historical significance can add considerable value to a coin. Coins that commemorate important events, figures, or eras often attract collectors who appreciate their historical context. The story behind a coin can make it more desirable, and this demand can drive prices up, especially for coins that have an interesting backstory.

The **market demand** for specific coins can fluctuate over time. Trends in collecting can shift, with certain coins becoming more sought after while others may lose their appeal. Keeping an eye on market trends can help you make better investment decisions, as understanding what collectors are currently interested in can guide your buying and selling strategies.

Provenance, or the history of ownership of a coin, can also affect its value. Coins with a well-documented history or those that have belonged to notable collectors can command higher prices. Collectors often value the story behind a coin just as much as the coin itself, which can significantly enhance its market appeal.

Another factor to consider is the **metal content** of the coin. Precious metals like gold, silver, and platinum have intrinsic value based on current market prices. Coins made from these metals can be worth more than their face value simply due to the metal content, especially during times of economic uncertainty when precious metals are in higher demand.

Authentication is critical in the world of coin collecting. Coins that have been professionally authenticated and graded by reputable organizations tend to have higher values. Collectors are often willing to pay a premium for coins that come with a guarantee of authenticity, as this reduces the risk of purchasing counterfeits.

Market conditions at the time of sale can also impact coin values. Economic factors, such as inflation or changes in the stock market, can influence how much collectors are willing to spend. Understanding the broader economic landscape can provide insights into when to buy or sell your coins for maximum profit.

Lastly, **collector sentiment** plays a subtle but vital role in determining coin value. Factors like emotional attachment, nostalgia, or community trends can affect how much collectors are willing to pay. Engaging with fellow collectors and participating in forums can provide insights into current sentiments and help you gauge the value of your collection.

In summary, several factors affect coin value, including rarity, condition, historical significance, market demand, provenance, metal content, authentication, market conditions, and collector sentiment. By understanding these elements, you can navigate the world of coin collecting with confidence, ensuring that your investments are both wise and rewarding.

Book 8: Transactions and Strategy

When it comes to **transactions** in the world of coin collecting, understanding the nuances of buying and selling is crucial. Whether you're a beginner or a seasoned collector, knowing how to navigate the marketplace can significantly impact the success of your collection. Start by establishing a clear **budget** for your transactions. This will help you avoid overspending and keep your collection focused on what truly interests you. Consider the long-term value of pieces you wish to acquire, as well as their potential for appreciation.

Research is your best friend. Before making a purchase, familiarize yourself with the **market trends** for the specific coins you're interested in. Websites, forums, and auction houses provide valuable insights into current values and demand. Don't hesitate to consult price guides or databases to get a sense of what constitutes a fair price. This knowledge will empower you to make informed decisions and negotiate effectively.

When you find a coin you want to purchase, always ask for **documentation** of authenticity. Reputable dealers will provide certificates or guarantees, which serve as proof that the coin is genuine. If a seller is unwilling to provide such documentation, it's a red flag. Additionally, consider the **return policy** of the seller. A fair return policy can provide peace of mind, especially for higher-value transactions.

Networking is another key element in successful transactions. Engage with fellow collectors at local shows and online forums. These connections can lead to valuable information about reputable dealers and upcoming sales. Sometimes, the best deals come from private collectors looking to sell directly, so being part of a community can open doors to unique opportunities.

When selling coins from your collection, presentation matters. Ensure that your coins are **clean** (but not overly polished) and well-documented. Provide potential buyers with all relevant information, including any certifications, grading details, and provenance. High-quality images can also enhance your listing, drawing in more interested buyers.

Consider the timing of your sales. Certain times of the year may yield better results, especially around major coin shows or events. Being aware of the **seasonal trends** in the market can help you decide when to sell. Additionally, if you're looking to sell online, platforms like eBay or specialized auction sites can help you reach a broader audience.

During negotiations, be prepared to stand firm on your price, but also be open to **reasonable offers**. Understanding the value of your coins and being confident in your asking price will help you navigate these discussions effectively. Remember, it's not just about making a sale; it's about building relationships within the community.Lastly, always keep an eye out for **scams** and red flags. If a deal seems too good to be true, it probably is. Trust your instincts and don't rush into any transaction without thorough consideration. Protect your investment by knowing the signs of counterfeit coins and fraudulent sellers.

11. Buying and Selling Coins

Stepping into the world of buying and selling coins can feel like entering a vibrant marketplace filled with history and potential. Imagine walking through rows of tables at a local coin show, each one laden with treasures waiting to be discovered. You might spot a gleaming silver dollar, its surface reflecting the overhead lights, or a vintage penny, its rich patina whispering tales of yesteryear. The excitement is palpable, but so are the challenges that come with navigating this intricate landscape.

When you decide to buy a coin, it's essential to approach the process with a blend of enthusiasm and caution. Picture yourself at a table, eyeing a coin that catches your attention. Before you make a decision, take a moment to engage the seller. Ask questions about the coin's history, its condition, and any provenance that might accompany it. A knowledgeable seller will appreciate your curiosity and be willing to provide details that can help you gauge the coin's authenticity and value. Remember, **trust is key** in any transaction, and establishing a rapport can lead to a more satisfying experience.

As you delve deeper into the buying process, consider the importance of **authentication**. In a world where counterfeits lurk, knowing how to verify a coin's legitimacy can save you from costly mistakes. Familiarizing yourself with common signs of authenticity—like weight, dimensions, and surface details—will empower you to make informed decisions. Additionally, don't hesitate to seek third-party grading services if you're uncertain. Investing in a professional opinion can provide peace of mind and bolster your collection's value.

Once you've acquired a few pieces, the time may come to sell. This phase can be equally thrilling and daunting. Imagine standing at a booth, ready to part with a cherished coin. The emotional weight of selling can be significant, especially if the coin holds memories or represents a milestone in your collecting journey. To ease this transition, think about your goals for the sale. Are you looking to upgrade your collection? Or perhaps you're hoping to cash in on an investment? Understanding your motivations will guide your approach and help you set a fair price.

When pricing your coins, do thorough research. Look at recent sales of similar items, consult price guides, and consider the current market trends. It's not uncommon for prices to fluctuate based on demand, so staying informed will help you strike the right balance between attracting buyers and maximizing your return. If you feel overwhelmed, consider enlisting the help of a reputable dealer who can provide insights on pricing strategies and market conditions.

As you navigate the selling process, be prepared for negotiations. Picture a friendly exchange where both parties are eager to reach a mutually beneficial agreement. Approach negotiations with an open mind and a willingness to listen. Remember, a successful sale often hinges on finding common ground. If a buyer expresses concerns about the price, engage in a dialogue to understand their perspective. This collaborative spirit can foster goodwill and lead to a successful transaction.

In the digital age, online platforms have transformed the way collectors buy and sell coins. Imagine scrolling through a vibrant marketplace on your computer screen, where thousands of listings beckon with the promise of rare finds. Online auctions and classified sites offer convenience and access to a broader audience, but they also come with their own set of challenges. The anonymity of the internet can make it difficult to assess trustworthiness, so always conduct thorough research on sellers and platforms before making a purchase.

When selling online, high-quality photographs are your best allies. A well-lit, detailed image can showcase a coin's unique features and attract potential buyers. Consider writing a compelling description that highlights the coin's history, condition, and any unique characteristics. This narrative approach not only informs buyers but also adds a personal touch that can resonate with collectors.

While online transactions can be efficient, don't underestimate the value of face-to-face interactions. Attending local coin shows or joining a numismatic club can provide invaluable opportunities to connect with fellow collectors and potential buyers. Picture yourself engaging in lively discussions, exchanging stories, and sharing your passion for coins. These connections can lead to fruitful transactions and lasting friendships.

As you embark on your buying and selling journey, always remain vigilant. The numismatic world, while filled with excitement, can also harbor pitfalls. Be wary of deals that seem too good to be true and always trust your instincts. If something feels off, it's worth pausing to reevaluate the situation. Your hard-earned money deserves careful consideration, and taking the time to make informed decisions will pay off in the long run.

Ultimately, the journey of buying and selling coins is not just about transactions; it's about building a collection that tells a story. Each coin you acquire adds a chapter to your narrative, and each sale can open new doors to future adventures. Embrace the process, engage with the community, and let your passion for numismatics guide you. With every coin you buy or sell, you're not just participating in a market—you're becoming part of a rich tapestry of history that connects collectors across generations.

How to Buy Coins: Dealers, Auctions, and Online

When it comes to buying coins, the journey can feel as intricate as the coins themselves. Imagine stepping into a bustling coin show, the air thick with excitement and the promise of discovery. Tables adorned with glimmering coins beckon you closer, each piece telling a story of history, craftsmanship, and value. However, amidst the allure, there lies a labyrinth of choices—dealers, auctions, and the vast world of online marketplaces. Each avenue offers its own set of opportunities and pitfalls, and understanding how to navigate them is crucial for any collector.

Let's start with **dealers**. These professionals can be your best allies in the quest for quality coins. A reputable dealer is not merely a seller; they are a wealth of knowledge, often possessing years of experience and a passion for numismatics. When you walk into a dealer's shop, take a moment to observe the atmosphere. Is it welcoming? Are the coins displayed with care? A well-organized shop reflects a dealer who respects their inventory and, by extension, their customers. Engage them in conversation. Ask about their favorite pieces or the stories behind certain coins. A good dealer will appreciate your curiosity and be eager to share their expertise.

As you build a rapport with your dealer, trust becomes a key element. Trust is not just about the coins you purchase; it's about the relationship you cultivate. A reputable dealer will be transparent about the coin's history, including its grade and any potential flaws. They should provide you with the necessary documentation or certification to assure you of the coin's authenticity. If a dealer seems evasive or unwilling to share information, it's a red flag. Remember, the goal is to create a collection that you can proudly pass down to future generations, and that begins with reliable sources.

Next, let's explore the realm of **auctions**. Auctions can be thrilling, offering the chance to acquire rare and unique pieces that may not be available through traditional dealers. Picture the excitement in the room as bidders raise their paddles, each vying for a coveted coin. However, participating in an auction requires a different mindset. Preparation is key. Before the auction, research the coins that interest you. Understand their market value and set a budget. It's easy to get swept up in the moment and exceed your limits, so having a clear plan is essential.

Once you've identified the coins you want, attend the auction preview. This is your opportunity to examine the coins up close. Look for signs of wear, check the details, and, if possible, compare them to similar pieces you've encountered. Authenticity is paramount, and you want to be sure you're bidding on a coin that meets your standards. Engage with the auctioneer and ask questions if you have any doubts. They should be willing to help you understand the coins being offered.

During the auction itself, maintain your composure. It can be easy to get caught up in the energy of the room, but staying calm will help you make rational decisions. If you find yourself in a bidding war, remember your budget. The thrill of the chase can sometimes cloud judgment, but the goal is to acquire coins that enhance your collection, not to win at all costs.

Now, let's not overlook the vast world of **online marketplaces**. The internet has revolutionized how collectors buy coins, providing access to a global inventory at the click of a button. However, this convenience comes with its own set of challenges. When browsing online, it's crucial to approach each listing with a discerning eye. Look for sellers with established reputations and positive reviews. Platforms that offer buyer protection can also provide peace of mind.

As you scroll through listings, take note of the photographs. High-quality images should clearly showcase the coin from multiple angles. If the seller only provides a single, blurry image, proceed with caution. Trust your instincts—if something feels off, it probably is. Additionally, read the descriptions carefully. A reputable seller will provide detailed information about the coin's condition, history, and any potential flaws. If the description is vague or overly optimistic, it may be a sign to look elsewhere.

When making a purchase online, don't hesitate to reach out to the seller with questions. A responsive and knowledgeable seller is often a good indicator of reliability. Ask about their return policy and what guarantees they offer regarding authenticity. This dialogue not only helps you make an informed decision but also establishes a connection that could benefit you in future transactions.

In your quest to build a remarkable coin collection, remember that each avenue—dealers, auctions, and online marketplaces—offers unique experiences and opportunities. Embrace the journey, and allow your passion for numismatics to guide you. Whether you're discovering a hidden gem at a local show or successfully bidding on a rare piece at an auction, each acquisition adds to the tapestry of your collection. And as you share your passion with your family, you'll create lasting memories that transcend generations.

Ultimately, the art of buying coins is not merely transactional; it's about building connections, honing your knowledge, and curating a collection that reflects your interests and values. So, step into the world of numismatics with confidence, and let your collection tell the story of your journey.

Selling Your Coins: Strategies and Tips

When the time comes to part with your coins, whether to make space for new acquisitions or to capitalize on your investment, the process can feel daunting. Selling coins is not just a transaction; it's a journey filled with emotional attachments and strategic decisions. It's essential to approach this process with both heart and head, ensuring that you maximize your returns while maintaining the integrity of your collection.

Imagine standing at a table at a local coin show, surrounded by fellow enthusiasts. You've spent years curating your collection, and now you're ready to sell a few pieces. The thrill of the hunt has been replaced by the anxiety of the sale. What's the right price? How do you find the right buyer? These questions swirl in your mind, but with the right strategies, you can navigate this landscape with confidence.

First, understanding the **value of your coins** is paramount. This isn't just about checking the latest price guides; it's about knowing the nuances of your specific coins. Factors such as rarity, demand, and condition play a significant role in determining their market value. Take the time to research comparable sales, perhaps by browsing online auction sites or consulting with dealers. This groundwork will arm you with the knowledge you need to set a realistic price.

Next, consider the **selling venues** available to you. Each option has its pros and cons, and the right choice will depend on your personal preferences and the nature of the coins you're selling. Online platforms like eBay can offer a wide audience, but they also come with fees and competition. Local coin shops provide a more personal touch but may offer lower prices due to their need to resell for profit. Coin shows can be an excellent middle ground, allowing you to interact directly with buyers and negotiate prices face-to-face.

As you prepare to sell, remember that presentation matters. High-quality photographs can make all the difference in attracting potential buyers, especially in online settings. Ensure your coins are clean and well-lit in the images you share. A well-crafted description that highlights the coin's history, condition, and unique features can also enhance its appeal. This isn't just a sale; it's a story you're sharing, and the more engaging that story, the more likely you are to find a buyer willing to pay a premium.

When it comes time to meet with potential buyers, whether at a show or in a private setting, **confidence is key**. Approach negotiations with a clear understanding of your coins' worth and a willingness to listen. Be prepared to answer questions about the provenance of your coins and any unique characteristics they may have. This knowledge not only builds trust but also reinforces your position as a knowledgeable collector.

It's also wise to be aware of **scams and pitfalls** that can occur during the selling process. Always ensure that you're dealing with reputable buyers, and don't hesitate to ask for references or check their history if you're unsure. If a deal seems too good to be true, it probably is. Trust your instincts and be prepared to walk away if something doesn't feel right. Your hard-earned collection deserves to be treated with respect.

As you navigate the selling process, consider the emotional aspect of parting with your coins. Each piece likely holds memories, stories, and a connection to your journey as a collector. It's natural to feel a sense of loss when selling, but remember that this is also an opportunity to pass on your passion. Perhaps you can share the story of your collection with the new owner, ensuring that the legacy of your coins continues.

Finally, after the sale, take a moment to reflect on the experience. What worked well? What could you improve for next time? Each sale is a learning opportunity, and as you refine your approach, you'll become more adept at navigating the world of coin selling. Whether you're selling to fund your next acquisition or simply to declutter, embrace the journey. Your collection is a reflection of your passion and dedication, and sharing it with others is just another way to celebrate that.

Avoiding Scams and Identifying Fakes

When you first step into the world of coin collecting, it can feel like diving into an intricate tapestry woven with history, culture, and, unfortunately, deception. The thrill of discovering a rare coin can be exhilarating, but it's essential to navigate this landscape with a discerning eye. As you embark on this journey, remember that the risk of encountering scams and counterfeit coins is ever-present. Let's explore the nuances of identifying fakes and safeguarding your collection.

Imagine attending a local coin show, the air thick with anticipation as collectors gather to share their passion. You spot a vendor showcasing a dazzling array of coins, each one seemingly more enticing than the last. Among them, a shimmering gold piece catches your eye. The vendor, with a charismatic smile, assures you of its authenticity and historical significance. But as you prepare to make a purchase, a nagging doubt creeps in. How can you be sure that this coin is not just a well-crafted imitation?

The first step in avoiding scams is to cultivate a healthy skepticism. It's not about being overly suspicious but rather about arming yourself with knowledge. Research is your best ally. Familiarize yourself with the characteristics of the coins you're interested in. For instance, if you're eyeing a specific vintage coin, study its design, weight, and any distinctive markings. Many reputable numismatic organizations offer resources online, including databases and forums where collectors share their experiences and insights. Engaging with these communities can provide invaluable guidance and a wealth of information.

As you delve deeper into the realm of coin collecting, you'll encounter various authentication techniques. One effective method is to learn about the specific minting processes used for different coins. For example, understanding how to identify the unique features of a coin minted in the 19th century versus a modern coin can significantly enhance your ability to spot a counterfeit. Pay attention to the edges, weight, and any inconsistencies in the design. Counterfeiters often overlook these details, and a keen eye can reveal discrepancies that may not be immediately obvious.

Another critical aspect of safeguarding your collection is to develop relationships with trusted dealers and experts. This doesn't mean you should rely solely on their expertise, but establishing a rapport can provide you with a safety net. A reputable dealer will not only offer genuine coins but also share insights about the market, trends, and potential pitfalls. They can act as mentors, guiding you through the complexities of the numismatic world. When you find a dealer you trust, it's like having a compass in uncharted territory.

It's also wise to invest in proper tools for authentication. Magnifying glasses and digital scales can be invaluable in your quest for authenticity. A magnifying glass allows you to examine the fine details of a coin, revealing imperfections that might indicate a fake. Similarly, weighing a coin can help you determine if it matches the standard weight for that particular type. Many counterfeit coins are slightly off in weight, a telltale sign that something is amiss.

As you navigate this intricate landscape, it's crucial to be aware of the common scams that plague the coin collecting community. One prevalent scheme involves counterfeit coins being sold at prices that seem too good to be true. If a deal appears overly generous, it often is. Remember, if something feels off, trust your instincts. It's better to walk away from a questionable deal than to risk tarnishing your collection.

Furthermore, consider documenting your collection meticulously. Keeping detailed records of each coin's purchase, including photographs and any relevant certificates of authenticity, can serve as a valuable resource in case you need to verify a coin's legitimacy later. This practice not only helps you maintain an organized collection but also builds a narrative that can be shared with your family, enriching the legacy you wish to pass down.

In your journey, you may also encounter situations where you're tempted to buy coins from online marketplaces. While these platforms can offer great deals, they also pose significant risks. Always do your due diligence before making a purchase. Research the seller's reputation, read reviews, and look for any red flags. If possible, request additional photographs or details about the coin. If the seller is unwilling to provide this information, it's a strong indication that you should proceed with caution.

As you gain experience, you'll develop a sixth sense for spotting fakes. This intuition comes from years of observation and learning. Attend local shows, engage with fellow collectors, and immerse yourself in the community. Each conversation, each coin you examine, adds to your knowledge and sharpens your instincts. Over time, you'll find that your confidence in identifying genuine coins grows, allowing you to enjoy the hobby without the constant shadow of doubt.

Ultimately, the goal of coin collecting goes beyond mere acquisition; it's about building a collection that tells a story, a collection that you can proudly share with your children. By investing time and effort into understanding the nuances of authenticity and scams, you're not just protecting your investment; you're creating a legacy. The coins you collect today will become the treasures you pass down, accompanied by the knowledge and passion for numismatics that you instill in the next generation.

In conclusion, the world of coin collecting is as rewarding as it is challenging. By arming yourself with knowledge, fostering relationships with trusted dealers, and honing your skills in authentication, you can navigate this intricate landscape with confidence. Remember, every coin has a story to tell, and with each addition to your collection, you're not just accumulating wealth; you're preserving history for future generations to cherish.

12. Investing in Coins

When it comes to investing in coins, the journey often begins with a spark of curiosity. Perhaps it's the allure of history encapsulated in a small piece of metal or the thrill of discovering a rare find at a local show. Whatever the initial draw, it's essential to approach coin investing with both passion and prudence. The world of numismatics is vast, and while it can be incredibly rewarding, it also requires a careful strategy to navigate successfully.

Many collectors start with an emotional connection to coins, often stemming from family traditions or personal stories. Imagine a father sharing tales of his childhood, recounting how he stumbled upon a silver dollar in his grandfather's attic. This connection to the past can ignite a lifelong passion for collecting, but it's crucial to remember that coin collecting is not merely a nostalgic hobby—it can also be a significant investment opportunity.

Understanding the market is the first step in this journey. Coin values fluctuate based on a variety of factors: rarity, demand, condition, and historical significance. For instance, a rare coin that once sold for a modest price can skyrocket in value when collectors begin to recognize its importance. Take the 1909-S V.D.B. Lincoln penny, for example. Once overlooked, it has become one of the most sought-after coins in the United States, with prices soaring to tens of thousands of dollars. This transformation illustrates the potential for substantial returns on investment.

However, investing in coins isn't just about chasing trends. It requires a deep understanding of the market and its nuances. Engaging with fellow collectors and experts can provide invaluable insights. Joining a local coin club or participating in online forums can help you gauge the current market climate and learn from seasoned investors. These interactions often lead to discussions about emerging trends or shifts in demand, which can be beneficial for making informed investment decisions.

As you delve deeper, consider the importance of **authentication**. The fear of acquiring a counterfeit coin is a genuine concern for many collectors. The market is rife with fakes, and without proper knowledge, even experienced investors can fall victim. Developing an eye for detail is essential. Familiarize yourself with the characteristics of genuine coins, such as weight, dimensions, and mint marks. Investing in a reputable authentication service can also provide peace of mind, ensuring that your investments are secure and legitimate.

Another critical aspect of coin investing is **diversification**. Just as in traditional investing, putting all your eggs in one basket can be risky. Consider building a collection that spans various types of coins— such as gold, silver, and historical pieces. This approach not only mitigates risk but also allows you to appreciate the vast spectrum of numismatics. Each coin tells a story, and a diverse collection can reflect the rich tapestry of history and culture.

Additionally, think about the long-term potential of your collection. Many collectors view their coins as a legacy to pass down to future generations. This perspective can shift your approach to investing. Instead of focusing solely on immediate financial gains, consider how each coin can contribute to a narrative that you can share with your children or grandchildren. This emotional connection can enhance the value of your collection beyond mere monetary worth.

As you grow more comfortable with your investments, stay informed about market trends and economic conditions. The value of coins can be influenced by broader economic factors, such as inflation or changes in precious metal prices. Keeping an eye on these trends can help you make strategic decisions about when to buy or sell. For example, during economic downturns, collectors may seek to liquidate assets, leading to increased availability of certain coins at lower prices. This could be an opportune time to expand your collection.

It's also essential to approach coin investing with a sense of patience. Unlike stocks or bonds, the coin market can be unpredictable. Prices may not rise immediately, and it's crucial to resist the temptation to sell hastily during market fluctuations. Instead, focus on the long-term value of your collection. Investing in coins is often a marathon, not a sprint. The patience you exercise can yield significant rewards as the market evolves and your collection matures.

Lastly, remember that the journey of coin collecting is as important as the destination. Each coin you acquire is a chapter in your story, filled with experiences, lessons, and memories. Embrace the excitement of the hunt, the joy of discovery, and the camaraderie of fellow collectors. This passion can transform what might initially seem like a financial investment into a fulfilling lifelong pursuit.

In conclusion, investing in coins offers a unique blend of history, passion, and potential financial return. By approaching it with a well-informed strategy, a commitment to authenticity, and an appreciation for the stories behind each piece, you can build a collection that not only enriches your life but also serves as a valuable legacy for future generations. As you embark on this journey, keep in mind that every coin is not just a piece of currency; it's a connection to the past, a reflection of the present, and a promise for the future.

Building a Valuable Collection

Building a valuable coin collection is akin to crafting a rich tapestry of history, culture, and personal significance. Each coin tells a story, and as a collector, you are the curator of these narratives. The journey of collecting is not merely about monetary value; it's about passion, knowledge, and the thrill of discovery. As you embark on this adventure, consider the elements that will transform your collection from a mere assortment of coins into a meaningful treasure trove.

First and foremost, **define your collecting goals**. Are you drawn to a specific era, geographical region, or type of coin? Perhaps you have a fascination with ancient civilizations, or maybe you're captivated by modern commemorative coins. Establishing a clear focus will guide your purchasing decisions and help you avoid the trap of impulse buys. Think of your collection as a puzzle; each piece should fit together to create a coherent picture. This intentionality will not only enhance your enjoyment but also increase the overall value of your collection.

As you refine your focus, **educate yourself** about the coins that pique your interest. Knowledge is your greatest ally in the world of numismatics. Dive into books, attend seminars, and engage with online forums where experienced collectors share their wisdom. Understanding the historical context, rarity, and condition of the coins will empower you to make informed decisions. Remember, a well-informed collector is less likely to fall prey to scams or counterfeit coins. Seek out reputable sources and don't hesitate to ask questions; the numismatic community is often eager to help newcomers.

When it comes to acquiring coins, **patience is key**. The thrill of the hunt can be intoxicating, but rushing into purchases often leads to regret. Take your time to research dealers, attend local coin shows, and explore online marketplaces. Each venue has its unique advantages and potential pitfalls. Building relationships with trusted dealers can also be invaluable; they can provide insights and access to rare finds that might not be available to the general public. As you navigate these avenues, keep an open mind but remain vigilant about authenticity and fair pricing.

Another vital aspect of building a valuable collection is **proper storage and preservation**. Coins are delicate artifacts, and their condition directly impacts their value. Invest in quality coin holders, such as acid-free flips or capsules, to protect your coins from environmental damage. Avoid cleaning coins, as this can diminish their value and ruin their aesthetic appeal. Instead, handle them with care, using gloves when necessary, and store them in a controlled environment. This attention to detail will ensure that your collection remains in pristine condition for years to come.

As your collection grows, so too should your understanding of **grading and valuation**. Familiarize yourself with the grading scales used in numismatics, as this knowledge will help you assess the quality of your coins and their potential market value. Whether you choose to have your coins professionally graded or prefer to grade them yourself, being able to accurately evaluate your collection is crucial. This skill not only enhances your confidence as a collector but also prepares you for future transactions.

One of the most rewarding aspects of coin collecting is the opportunity to **share your passion** with others. Involve your family in your hobby—teach your children about the history behind each coin, or take them to local shows. This not only creates lasting memories but also instills a sense of appreciation for history and craftsmanship in the younger generation. Consider organizing family coin nights where you can discuss recent acquisitions or research interesting coins together. This shared experience can deepen your familial bonds and ensure that your love for collecting is passed down.

In your pursuit of building a valuable collection, remember that it's not solely about the coins themselves, but also about the **stories they carry**. Each coin has a unique history, whether it was minted during a significant historical event or represents a cultural milestone. Seek out the tales behind your coins; these narratives will enrich your collection and provide you with engaging stories to share with fellow collectors and family members alike.

As you reflect on your collecting journey, **remain adaptable**. The world of numismatics is ever-evolving, with trends and interests shifting over time. Stay informed about market developments and emerging areas of interest within the community. This flexibility will not only enhance your collecting experience but also position you to make savvy investment decisions as you build your collection.

Ultimately, building a valuable coin collection is a deeply personal endeavor. It's about curating a reflection of your interests, values, and passions. As you navigate this exciting world, embrace the challenges and triumphs that come with it. Each coin you acquire is a step toward creating a legacy that you can share with future generations—a testament to your dedication and love for the art of collecting.

Understanding Investment Potential

When diving into the world of numismatics, the allure of investment potential can be as captivating as the coins themselves. Collectors often find themselves at a crossroads: Is this hobby merely a passion, or can it also be a prudent investment? Understanding how to navigate this landscape requires more than just an appreciation for history; it demands a strategic mindset.

Consider the journey of a collector who began with a simple interest in coins. At first, it was about the thrill of the hunt—scouring flea markets, estate sales, and local shows for hidden treasures. Each coin carried its own story, a piece of history waiting to be uncovered. But as this collector delved deeper, the realization dawned that some coins were not just artifacts of the past; they were also valuable assets. This duality sparked a new layer of enthusiasm, transforming a casual hobby into a calculated investment.

As our collector began to explore the investment potential of their collection, they discovered that certain coins, especially those with historical significance or rarity, could appreciate significantly over time. The key was understanding which coins held value and why. For instance, a rare mint error coin might fetch a price far beyond its face value, while a common coin, no matter how well-preserved, might remain just that—a common coin. This realization prompted a deeper dive into the factors that influence coin value.

The journey of understanding investment potential is often marked by learning about market trends. Just as the stock market fluctuates, so too does the value of coins. For instance, the popularity of certain series can wax and wane, influenced by factors such as collector demand, historical anniversaries, or even media coverage. Our collector learned to keep an eye on auction results and price guides, not merely as a means of valuation but as a way to anticipate market movements. Engaging with fellow collectors and industry experts became essential. Conversations at local shows and online forums provided insights that no price guide could offer alone.

However, investment in coins is not without its risks. The fear of counterfeits looms large, especially for those looking to invest substantial sums. Our collector faced this challenge head-on by educating themselves on authentication techniques. They learned to recognize the subtle differences between a genuine coin and a counterfeit, seeking out resources and communities where experienced collectors shared their knowledge. This proactive approach not only enhanced their confidence but also fortified their collection against potential pitfalls.

Moreover, the collector began to appreciate the importance of diversification within their collection. Just as an investor would not place all their capital in a single stock, it's wise for a coin collector to explore various types of coins. This might include a mix of gold and silver bullion, historical coins, and modern commemoratives. Each category brings its own set of risks and rewards, and understanding this balance is crucial for long-term success.

As the collector's knowledge deepened, they realized that the investment potential of their collection also hinged on emotional factors. Coins are not just financial instruments; they are tangible pieces of history that evoke memories and stories. This emotional connection can enhance the value of a collection in ways that transcend market trends. For our collector, the coins they chose to invest in were often tied to personal milestones or family heritage, adding layers of significance that were not strictly financial.

Furthermore, as the collector contemplated the future, thoughts of legacy began to emerge. They envisioned passing down their collection to their children, imparting not just the coins themselves but the stories and lessons learned along the way. This desire to create a lasting legacy added a poignant dimension to their collecting journey. It became evident that the investment potential of their collection was not solely about monetary gain; it was also about creating a family heirloom, a tangible connection to the past that could inspire future generations.

In the end, understanding the investment potential of coin collecting is a multifaceted endeavor. It requires a blend of passion, education, and strategy. As our collector continued to refine their approach, they found that the journey was as rewarding as the destination. Each coin became a chapter in their story, a testament to their growing expertise and a reflection of their values. In navigating the world of numismatics, they discovered that the true treasure lay not just in the coins themselves, but in the knowledge, connections, and memories forged along the way.

Long-Term Storage and Preservation

As you embark on the rewarding journey of coin collecting, the significance of proper long-term storage and preservation cannot be overstated. Your collection is not merely a collection of metal; it is a tapestry of history, culture, and personal investment. Each coin tells a story, and how you care for these treasures will determine whether those stories endure for generations to come.

Imagine stumbling upon a rare coin that resonates with your personal history or one that could potentially be worth a small fortune. The excitement is palpable, yet the thrill can quickly dissipate if that coin is not stored correctly. The harsh reality is that environmental factors can wreak havoc on unprotected coins, leading to corrosion, tarnishing, or worse—irreparable damage. This is where understanding the essentials of storage and preservation becomes paramount.

First and foremost, consider the environment in which you store your coins. Humidity is a silent enemy; too much moisture can lead to the formation of rust and tarnish, while an excessively dry environment can cause coins to become brittle. Ideally, you want to maintain a stable humidity level between 30% and 50%. Investing in a hygrometer can help you monitor these levels effectively. If you find that your space tends to fluctuate, consider using a dehumidifier or a humidifier to keep conditions optimal.

Temperature is another critical factor. Coins should ideally be stored in a cool, stable environment, away from direct sunlight. Fluctuating temperatures can cause metals to expand and contract, potentially leading to stress fractures. A temperature range of 65°F to 70°F is generally considered ideal for long-term storage. Avoid placing your collection near heat sources, such as radiators or vents, where temperature changes are frequent.

Next, let's talk about the materials you use for storage. Many collectors opt for coin holders, albums, or storage boxes that are specifically designed for numismatics. These products are often made from materials that are inert and won't react with the coins over time. For instance, avoid PVC holders, as they can cause damage due to the chemicals they release. Instead, look for holders made of mylar, which is safe for long-term storage. When handling your coins, always use cotton gloves. The natural oils and dirt from your fingers can leave residues that lead to tarnishing.

As you curate your collection, consider the categorization of your coins. You might choose to store them by type, year, or even by the story each coin tells. This not only makes it easier to locate specific pieces but also adds a personal touch to your collection. Imagine sharing these stories with your children or grandchildren, passing down not just coins but the rich narratives behind each one. This connection can foster a deeper appreciation for the art of collecting and the history encapsulated in each piece.

In addition to the physical aspects of storage, consider the documentation of your collection. Keeping a detailed inventory of your coins, including their purchase price, condition, and any relevant history, is invaluable. This record not only helps you keep track of your collection but can also serve as a crucial reference when it comes time to appraise or sell your coins. You may want to include photographs of each coin, as visual documentation can be beneficial for insurance purposes and can enhance the story you tell about your collection.

As you navigate the world of coin collecting, you may encounter situations that challenge your commitment to preservation. Perhaps you come across a coin that you are tempted to clean, believing that a little polish will restore its luster. However, it is crucial to resist this temptation. Cleaning coins can often do more harm than good, stripping away valuable patina and potentially reducing the coin's worth. Instead, focus on preserving the natural beauty and history of each piece. If you are unsure about a coin's condition, consult with a professional numismatist who can provide guidance on the best course of action.

In your journey, you may also consider insurance for your collection. While it may seem excessive, protecting your investment is wise, especially as your collection grows. Speak with an insurance agent who specializes in collectibles to understand how best to insure your coins, ensuring that they are covered in case of theft, loss, or damage.

Finally, remember that coin collecting is not just about the coins themselves; it's about the community and the connections you build along the way. Engage with fellow collectors, attend local shows, and participate in forums where you can share your experiences and learn from others. This interaction not only enriches your knowledge but also enhances the joy of collecting. The stories you exchange and the friendships you forge can add another layer of significance to your collection.

As you continue to build your collection, keep in mind that proper long-term storage and preservation are not merely practical considerations; they are an integral part of your journey as a collector. By safeguarding your coins, you are honoring their history and ensuring that the legacy of your collection can be shared with future generations. So, invest the time and effort into creating a safe and nurturing environment for your coins, and watch as your collection flourishes, becoming a cherished part of your family's story.

Book 9: Advanced Topics in Numismatics

As you delve deeper into the world of numismatics, you'll encounter a variety of advanced topics that can significantly enhance your understanding and appreciation of coin collecting. This chapter aims to equip you with knowledge that goes beyond the basics, focusing on the intricacies and nuances that every serious collector should know.

Understanding Coin Grading

Coin grading is a critical aspect of numismatics, as it directly affects a coin's value. The **Sheldon Scale**, ranging from 1 to 70, is the most widely used grading system. A coin graded 70 is considered perfect, while a grade of 1 indicates a heavily worn coin. Familiarizing yourself with this scale will help you make informed purchasing decisions and assess the quality of your collection.

When grading coins, consider factors such as **strike**, **luster**, **color**, and **surface quality**. Each of these elements plays a vital role in determining a coin's grade. For instance, a coin with a strong strike and brilliant luster will typically receive a higher grade than one with a weak strike and dull appearance. Understanding these criteria will not only enhance your grading skills but also bolster your confidence when discussing coins with fellow collectors.

Market Trends and Investment Strategies

Staying abreast of **market trends** is essential for anyone looking to invest in numismatics. The value of coins can fluctuate based on various factors, including economic conditions, collector demand, and changes in the market. Regularly reviewing auction results, attending coin shows, and participating in online forums can provide valuable insights into current market dynamics.

When considering investment strategies, it's crucial to diversify your collection. Focus on acquiring coins from various categories, such as **gold**, **silver**, and **historical coins**. This diversification will not only minimize risk but also enhance your collection's overall appeal. Additionally, consider investing in coins that have a strong historical significance or are part of popular series, as these tend to retain value better over time.

Authentication Techniques

One of the most pressing concerns for collectors is the fear of **counterfeit coins**. With the rise of sophisticated counterfeiting techniques, it's imperative to arm yourself with the knowledge necessary for authenticating your coins. Start by familiarizing yourself with the specific characteristics of genuine coins, including **weight**, **size**, and **design elements**.Investing in tools such as a **digital scale** and a **microscope** can aid in the authentication process. Additionally, consider seeking the help of professional grading services that offer authentication as part of their evaluation. This not only provides peace of mind but also adds credibility to your collection.

Engaging with the Numismatic Community

Engagement with the numismatic community can greatly enrich your collecting experience. Whether through **online forums**, local coin clubs, or national shows, connecting with other collectors allows you to share knowledge, trade coins, and gain insights into best practices. Participating in discussions can also help you stay informed about new developments in the field.Don't hesitate to attend workshops or seminars offered by experienced collectors or industry experts. These events can provide invaluable information and enhance your understanding of complex topics. Building relationships within the community can also lead to potential trading opportunities and collaborations on future collecting ventures.

Preservation and Storage of Your Collection

Proper preservation and storage of your coins are paramount to maintaining their condition and value. Invest in **high-quality storage solutions** such as coin holders, capsules, and albums specifically designed for numismatics. Avoid using PVC-based materials, as they can damage coins over time. Instead, opt for acid-free products that provide a safe environment for your collection.Additionally, consider the environmental factors in your storage area. Coins should be kept in a stable environment, away from extreme temperatures, humidity, and direct sunlight. Regularly inspecting your collection for signs of damage or deterioration will help ensure that your coins remain in optimal condition for years to come.

Exploring International Coinage

While North American coins are often the focus of many collectors, exploring **international coinage** can broaden your horizons and add depth to your collection. Each country has its own unique history and coinage traditions, offering a variety of designs, metals, and denominations. Researching the history and significance of foreign coins can provide fascinating insights and enhance your overall appreciation of numismatics.Consider focusing on specific regions or themes, such as **colonial coins**, **ancient coins**, or **coins from emerging markets**. This targeted approach can make your collecting journey more rewarding and allow you to connect with other collectors who share similar interests.

Legacy and Family Involvement

As you build your collection, think about the legacy you wish to leave behind. Involving your family in your numismatic pursuits can create lasting memories and instill an appreciation for history and craftsmanship in future generations. Share your knowledge with your children or grandchildren, encouraging them to participate in the hobby. Consider hosting family coin nights, where you can discuss your collection and engage in fun activities related to numismatics.Documenting your collection with notes on each coin's history, significance, and your personal experiences can also serve as a meaningful legacy. This not only helps educate future collectors but also provides a tangible connection to your passion for coin collecting.

13. Advanced Strategies for Collectors

As you delve deeper into the world of numismatics, it's essential to explore **advanced strategies** that can elevate your collecting experience and enhance the value of your collection. This section will provide you with insights and techniques that cater to more seasoned collectors, focusing on how to navigate the complexities of the market while ensuring that your collection remains both personally fulfilling and financially sound.

Building Relationships with Dealers

Establishing strong relationships with **trusted dealers** can significantly benefit your collecting journey. These connections can lead to exclusive access to rare coins, better pricing, and invaluable insights into market trends. Here are some tips for fostering these relationships:

- **Attend local coin shows** and events regularly to meet dealers in person. Building rapport face-to-face can lead to trust and future opportunities.

- **Communicate openly** about your collecting interests and goals. This transparency allows dealers to provide tailored recommendations that align with your objectives.

- **Be respectful** of their time and expertise. Acknowledging their knowledge fosters goodwill and can lead to better service in the long run.

Diversifying Your Collection

Diversification is not just a strategy for investment portfolios; it applies to coin collecting as well. By expanding the types of coins in your collection, you can mitigate risks and increase potential rewards. Consider the following:

- **Explore different eras** and geographical regions. Collecting coins from various historical periods or countries can enhance the richness of your collection.

- **Incorporate different types** of coins, such as commemorative coins, bullion, or error coins. This variety can make your collection more interesting and appealing to future buyers.

- **Stay informed** about emerging trends in the numismatic world. New collecting niches can provide unique opportunities for investment and personal satisfaction.

Investment Strategies

While many collectors enjoy coins for their beauty and historical significance, viewing your collection through an investment lens can yield financial benefits. Here are strategies to consider:

- **Research market trends** to understand which coins are appreciating in value. Keeping an eye on auction results and price guides can help you make informed purchasing decisions.

- **Consider the condition** of coins as a critical factor in their value. Learning to grade coins accurately will allow you to assess whether a coin is a good investment.

- **Think long-term**. Investing in coins should be approached with patience, as the market can fluctuate. Focus on acquiring pieces that you believe will appreciate over time.

Utilizing Technology

The digital age has transformed the way collectors engage with the hobby. Leveraging technology can enhance your collecting experience:

- **Join online forums** and communities where you can exchange information, ask questions, and share experiences with fellow collectors. These platforms can be invaluable for learning and networking.

- **Use mobile apps** for tracking your collection and managing your inventory. Many apps provide features for grading, pricing, and even photographing your coins.

- **Stay updated** with online resources. Websites dedicated to numismatics can offer articles, videos, and webinars that keep you informed about the latest developments in the field.

Participating in Auctions

Auctions can be an exciting way to acquire rare coins, but they require a strategic approach. Here are some tips for participating effectively:

- **Research auction houses** to find reputable ones with a strong track record. Understanding their bidding processes and fees is crucial to avoid surprises.

- **Set a budget** before participating. It's easy to get caught up in the excitement of bidding, so having a clear financial limit helps maintain discipline.

- **Inspect coins** whenever possible before bidding. This hands-on approach gives you a better understanding of the coin's condition and authenticity.

Documenting Your Collection

Keeping detailed records of your collection is not only useful for personal enjoyment but also essential for future transactions and appraisals:

- **Maintain a log** of each coin, including its purchase date, price, condition, and any relevant history. This documentation can enhance your collection's value.

- **Photograph your coins** for visual records. High-quality images can be helpful for insurance purposes and when considering selling or trading your coins.

- **Consider creating a digital portfolio** that showcases your collection. This can be a great way to share your passion with family, friends, and fellow collectors.

Engaging with the Community

Being part of the numismatic community can enrich your collecting experience. Engaging with others who share your passion can lead to knowledge sharing and potential partnerships:

- **Join local coin clubs** to meet fellow collectors and participate in discussions, events, and educational programs.

- **Volunteer at coin shows** or events. This involvement can deepen your understanding of the hobby and expand your network.

- **Share your story** and experiences through blogs or social media. Contributing to the community can position you as a knowledgeable collector and help others in their journeys.

Passing Down Your Collection

As you build your collection, consider its future legacy. Involving your family can create lasting memories and ensure your passion continues:

- **Involve your children** in the collecting process. Teaching them about coins can foster their interest and appreciation for the hobby.

- **Document your collection's history** to share with future generations. This narrative can add sentimental value and context to your coins.

- **Discuss your plans** for the collection openly with your family. Ensuring they understand its significance can help them appreciate and care for it after you pass it down.

By embracing these advanced strategies, you can navigate the world of coin collecting with confidence and purpose. Whether you are enhancing your investment approach, expanding your knowledge, or deepening your connections within the community, these insights will help you build a collection that is not only financially rewarding but also rich in personal significance.

Specialization and Focus Areas

When embarking on your journey in coin collecting, it's essential to determine your **specialization**. A focused approach allows you to build a collection that not only reflects your interests but also enhances your expertise in specific areas of numismatics. Specializing can make the collecting process more enjoyable and rewarding.

One popular area of specialization is **historical coins**. These are coins that have significant historical relevance, often tied to pivotal events, cultures, or figures. Collecting historical coins can provide insights into the past and a tangible connection to history. This specialization often involves researching the stories behind each coin, enriching your understanding of different eras and civilizations.

Another specialization is **error coins**. These are coins that have been minted with mistakes, such as double strikes or misaligned designs. Error coins can be particularly fascinating because they often have a limited supply, making them highly sought after by collectors. Understanding the nuances of error coins requires a keen eye and a commitment to learning about minting processes.

Modern coins are also a popular choice for collectors. This includes coins minted in the last few decades, often featuring innovative designs and themes. Modern coins can be easier to acquire than older coins, and many collectors appreciate the contemporary artistry involved. Additionally, modern coins often have lower prices, making them accessible for beginners.

If you have an interest in **precious metals**, consider specializing in bullion coins. These coins are valued based on their metal content rather than their numismatic value. Collecting bullion coins can be a strategic investment, as they often retain intrinsic value over time. Understanding market trends for precious metals can enhance your investment strategy.

World coins present another exciting avenue for specialization. Collecting coins from different countries allows you to explore diverse cultures and economies. World coins can vary significantly in design, material, and historical context, providing a rich tapestry for collectors to appreciate. This specialization often requires knowledge of international coinage and the ability to navigate various market conditions.

For the environmentally conscious collector, **commemorative coins** can be particularly appealing. These coins are minted to celebrate specific events, anniversaries, or causes. Commemorative coins often feature unique designs and limited mintage, making them attractive to collectors. This specialization allows you to support causes that resonate with you while building a meaningful collection.

As you consider your specialization, think about your **personal interests** and what aspects of coin collecting excite you the most. Whether it's the thrill of discovering a rare error coin or the joy of connecting with history through ancient coins, your passion will guide your collecting journey. Remember, specialization not only enhances your knowledge but also enriches your experience as a collector.

Moreover, engaging with a community of collectors can deepen your understanding of your chosen specialization. Whether through online forums, local clubs, or coin shows, sharing insights and experiences can lead to valuable connections and learning opportunities. This community engagement can also provide support and resources as you navigate the complexities of your specialization.

Ultimately, your specialization should align with your **long-term goals** as a collector. Consider how you want your collection to evolve over time. Are you looking to build a legacy to pass down to your children, or are you primarily focused on investment potential? Understanding your objectives will help you make informed decisions as you develop your collection.

In summary, choosing a specialization in coin collecting is a personal journey that can greatly enhance your experience. By focusing on a specific area, you can deepen your knowledge, connect with like-minded individuals, and build a collection that reflects your interests and values. Embrace the adventure of specialization, and let your passion for numismatics guide you.

Building Exhibit-Quality Collections

Creating an exhibit-quality collection is a journey that transcends mere accumulation; it embodies the passion and dedication of a collector. To build a collection that not only impresses but also tells a story, one must consider several essential elements that elevate it from the ordinary to the extraordinary.

Understanding Your Theme

The first step in building an exhibit-quality collection is defining a **theme**. This could revolve around a specific era, type of coin, or even a historical event. A well-defined theme helps to create a cohesive narrative that resonates with viewers. For instance, a collection focused on **ancient coins** can illustrate the evolution of currency over centuries, while a collection of **commemorative coins** can highlight significant milestones in history.

Quality Over Quantity

In the world of numismatics, the **quality** of coins is paramount. Aspiring collectors should prioritize acquiring coins that are in excellent condition, even if it means having fewer pieces in the collection. Look for coins with high **grade ratings** and minimal wear. A single high-quality coin can often be more valuable and visually striking than several lower-quality pieces.

Documentation and Provenance

Every coin in your collection should come with a thorough **documentation** of its provenance. This includes details about its history, previous ownership, and any relevant certificates of authenticity. Not only does this enhance the value of your coins, but it also adds to the story you can share with others. Potential buyers or fellow collectors will appreciate the transparency and depth of information.

Presentation Matters

The way you present your collection can significantly impact its perception. Invest in **high-quality display cases** that protect your coins while allowing them to shine. Consider using **acrylic holders** or **coin albums** that are acid-free to prevent any damage over time. A well-organized display can captivate viewers and enhance their appreciation of the collection.

Engaging the Audience

When showcasing your collection, think about how to engage your audience. Consider providing **informative labels** for each coin, detailing its significance, history, and any interesting anecdotes. This not only educates viewers but also invites them to connect with the collection on a deeper level.

Sharing personal stories about how you acquired certain coins can also create a more relatable experience.

Networking and Community Involvement

Building an exhibit-quality collection is not just about the coins; it's also about the **community** you engage with. Attend local coin shows, join numismatic clubs, and participate in online forums. Networking with fellow collectors can provide valuable insights, opportunities for trades, and access to rare coins. The relationships you build can be just as rewarding as the collection itself.

Continuous Learning

The world of numismatics is ever-evolving, with new discoveries and trends emerging regularly. To maintain the quality of your collection, commit to **continuous learning**. Stay updated on market trends, authentication techniques, and new technologies in coin grading. Resources like books, workshops, and online courses can enhance your knowledge and help you make informed decisions.

Preserving Your Collection

Proper **preservation** techniques are crucial for maintaining the integrity of your collection. Keep your coins in a controlled environment, avoiding exposure to humidity, temperature fluctuations, and direct sunlight. Regularly inspect your coins for any signs of damage or deterioration, and address any issues promptly to ensure their longevity.

Sharing Your Passion

Finally, consider the legacy you wish to leave behind. Involve your family in your collecting journey to create lasting memories and foster a shared passion for numismatics. Hosting family events or educational sessions can not only enrich your own experience but also inspire the next generation of collectors to appreciate the value of history and craftsmanship in coins.

By focusing on these key elements, you can create an exhibit-quality collection that not only showcases your dedication to numismatics but also stands as a testament to the stories and histories encapsulated within each coin. Remember, it's not just about the coins themselves; it's about the journey, the connections, and the legacy you build along the way.

Numismatic Literature and Research

Numismatic literature is an invaluable resource for anyone interested in coin collecting, providing insights, historical context, and practical guidance. Whether you are a novice or an experienced collector, understanding the breadth of available literature can significantly enhance your collecting journey.

Types of Numismatic Literature

Numismatic literature encompasses a variety of formats, each serving different purposes. **Books**, **magazines**, and **online resources** are just a few examples. Each type can cater to specific needs, such as historical research, valuation, or authentication.

Books

Books are fundamental to numismatic research. They range from comprehensive guides on specific coin types to detailed histories of coinage in various cultures. Look for titles that are well-reviewed and authored by reputable numismatists. **Essential reference books** include catalogs, grading guides, and historical accounts, which not only provide information but also enrich your understanding of the coins you collect.

Magazines

Numismatic magazines offer a dynamic way to stay updated on trends, market values, and new discoveries in the field. Publications such as **Coin World** and **Numismatic News** feature articles from industry experts, auction results, and tips for collectors. Subscribing to these magazines can keep you informed and connected to the numismatic community.

Online Resources

The internet has revolutionized access to numismatic literature. Websites, forums, and digital libraries provide vast amounts of information at your fingertips. Websites like **Numismatic Guaranty Corporation (NGC)** and **American Numismatic Association (ANA)** offer educational resources, articles, and forums for collectors to share experiences. Utilizing these platforms can enhance your knowledge and provide a sense of community.

Research Techniques

When diving into numismatic literature, adopting effective research techniques is crucial. Start by identifying your specific interests or questions, which will guide your reading. **Taking notes** while reading can help you retain important information and create a personal reference guide. Additionally, consider joining local or online numismatic clubs, where you can discuss literature and share insights with fellow collectors.

Evaluating Sources

Not all numismatic literature is created equal. It's important to evaluate the credibility of your sources. Look for **peer-reviewed publications**, books authored by recognized experts, and articles that cite reputable references. This diligence ensures that the information you gather is accurate and reliable, helping you avoid potential pitfalls in your collecting journey.

Incorporating Literature into Your Collection

As you build your collection, integrating numismatic literature into your practice can be immensely beneficial. Use books and articles to **guide your purchasing decisions**, understand the historical significance of your coins, and learn about grading standards. This knowledge not only enhances your collecting experience but also empowers you to make informed decisions.

Building a Personal Library

Creating a personal library of numismatic literature can serve as a valuable resource for years to come. Start with foundational texts, then expand into specialized areas that interest you. Organize your collection in a way that makes it easy to reference, and don't hesitate to annotate your books with personal insights or notes. This library will become a testament to your journey as a collector.

Engaging with Authors and Experts

Many authors and experts in numismatics are approachable and willing to share their knowledge. Attend lectures, workshops, or book signings to engage directly with these individuals. This interaction can provide deeper insights and foster connections within the numismatic community. **Networking** with these experts can also lead to recommendations for further reading and research.

In summary, numismatic literature is a cornerstone of successful coin collecting. By exploring various types of literature, employing effective research techniques, and integrating this knowledge into your collecting practices, you can enhance your understanding and appreciation of the hobby. As you continue to build your collection and pass it down to future generations, the insights gained from numismatic literature will undoubtedly enrich the legacy you create.

14. Coin Authentication and Security

When it comes to **coin authentication**, understanding the basics is crucial for any collector. The world of numismatics is filled with intricate details that can make or break a collection. The first step in ensuring the authenticity of your coins is to become familiar with the specific characteristics of the coins you are collecting. This includes knowing the **mint marks**, **design elements**, and **weight specifications** that are unique to each coin type.One effective method for verifying authenticity is to **compare your coins** with high-quality images from reputable sources. Online databases and numismatic catalogs can be invaluable tools in this process. Look for discrepancies in details such as **edge lettering**, **die marks**, and **overall condition**. If something seems off, it's worth further investigation.

Another essential aspect of authentication is **physical examination**. Use tools like a jeweler's loupe or a microscope to inspect the coin closely. Look for signs of wear, scratches, or any alterations that may indicate a counterfeit. Additionally, familiarize yourself with the **sound test**; different metals produce distinct sounds when dropped. This can sometimes help identify fakes, especially when dealing with older coins.In recent years, technology has advanced significantly in the field of coin authentication. **Professional grading services** now utilize sophisticated methods, including X-ray fluorescence (XRF) and laser scanning, to determine a coin's authenticity. While these services often come at a cost, they provide a level of assurance that is invaluable, especially for high-value coins.

Moreover, it's essential to stay informed about the latest trends in counterfeiting. Scammers are becoming increasingly adept at creating convincing replicas. Join **numismatic forums** or local clubs to share information about known counterfeit coins and learn from the experiences of other collectors. Engaging with a community can significantly enhance your knowledge and help you avoid potential pitfalls.When purchasing coins, always consider the **reputation of the seller**. Whether you're buying from a dealer, at a show, or online, it's vital to ensure that the seller has a good track record. Ask for references or check online reviews. A reputable dealer will often provide a guarantee of authenticity, which can offer peace of mind.

Documenting your collection is another critical step in maintaining its integrity. Keep detailed records of each coin, including purchase dates, prices, and sources. This not only helps in verifying authenticity but also aids in **insurance evaluations** should anything happen to your collection.

As you build your collection, consider investing in a few **authentication tools** for your home. A simple digital scale can help you check the weight of coins, while a magnet can be used to test for ferromagnetic materials that should not be present in certain coins. These tools can provide an extra layer of security when assessing new additions to your collection.Lastly, always trust your instincts. If a deal seems too good to be true, it probably is. The world of coin collecting is filled with opportunities, but it also has its share of risks. By arming yourself with knowledge and staying vigilant, you can enjoy your hobby with confidence, knowing that your collection is both authentic and valuable.

Identifying Counterfeits

In the world of coin collecting, one of the most daunting challenges is **identifying counterfeits**. As a collector, whether you're just starting or have years of experience, the fear of purchasing a fake coin can be overwhelming. This section aims to equip you with the knowledge and tools necessary to recognize genuine coins and avoid the pitfalls of counterfeiting.The first step in identifying counterfeits is to **understand the common types of counterfeit coins**. There are primarily two categories: **cast counterfeits** and **struck counterfeits**. Cast counterfeits are made by pouring molten metal into a mold, while struck counterfeits are created by using a die to stamp the image onto a blank coin. Each type has its own telltale signs that can help you discern authenticity.

When examining a coin, start by **analyzing its weight and dimensions**. Genuine coins have specific weight and size specifications. A counterfeit coin may feel lighter or heavier than it should. Invest in a quality scale that can measure in grams and a set of calipers to check the diameter and thickness. This simple step can often save you from a costly mistake.Next, examine the **design details**. Genuine coins have distinct features that are often hard to replicate perfectly. Look closely at the details of the coin, such as the lettering, the edges, and the relief. Counterfeit coins often have blurred details or uneven surfaces. Use a magnifying glass to inspect the coin closely; this can reveal inconsistencies that might not be visible to the naked eye.Another critical aspect is to **check for mint marks**. Mint marks indicate where a coin was produced and can be crucial in identifying its authenticity. Familiarize yourself with the mint marks of the coins you collect. Counterfeit coins may have incorrect or missing mint marks, which can be a red flag.

Additionally, consider the **coin's patina**. Genuine coins develop a natural patina over time, which can affect their color and sheen. A shiny, new-looking coin may indicate a counterfeit, especially if it's supposed to be an older piece. Use your knowledge of the coin's history to assess whether its condition aligns with its age.Utilizing **professional resources** is also invaluable. Don't hesitate to consult with experts or use reputable authentication services. Many organizations provide third-party grading and authentication, which can give you peace of mind. Remember, investing in professional opinions is often worth the cost, especially for high-value coins.In addition to these tips, keep an eye out for **recent trends in counterfeiting**. The methods used by counterfeiters are constantly evolving, and staying informed can help you avoid falling victim to new techniques. Joining forums or attending local coin shows can provide insights and updates from fellow collectors and experts.

Finally, always trust your **instincts**. If something feels off about a coin, it's better to err on the side of caution. Take your time, do your research, and don't rush into a purchase. Building a collection is a journey, and ensuring the authenticity of your coins is a crucial part of that process.By following these guidelines and remaining vigilant, you can confidently navigate the world of coin collecting, ensuring that your collection is both authentic and valuable. Remember, the goal is to create a collection that not only holds financial value but also carries historical significance—a legacy you can proudly pass down to future generations.

Security Techniques and Tools

When it comes to securing your coin collection, employing the right techniques and tools can make all the difference. The world of numismatics is not just about collecting; it's also about protecting your investments. Here are several essential strategies to ensure your collection remains safe and sound.

Physical Security Measures

Start with the basics of **physical security**. This includes keeping your collection in a secure location within your home. Consider using a **safe** or a **lockbox** that is both fireproof and waterproof. This not only protects your coins from theft but also from unforeseen disasters.

Additionally, make sure to **limit access** to your collection. Only share information about your collection with trusted individuals. The fewer people who know about your collection, the less likely it is to attract unwanted attention.

Insurance Considerations

Having the right insurance is crucial for any collector. Look into **specialized insurance policies** that cover collectibles. Regular homeowner's insurance may not adequately protect your coins against theft or damage. Ensure that you have a detailed **inventory** of your coins, including photographs and appraisals, to facilitate any claims in the event of a loss.

Environmental Controls

Coins are sensitive to their environment. To maintain their condition, store them in a climate-controlled area. Avoid **extreme temperatures** and humidity, as these can lead to tarnishing and corrosion. Consider using **dehumidifiers** in damp areas and ensuring proper ventilation.

Handling Techniques

When handling coins, always use **clean hands** or wear cotton gloves. Oils and dirt from your fingers can cause damage over time. Hold coins by the edges rather than the faces to avoid scratches and wear. If you need to clean a coin, be cautious; improper cleaning can significantly reduce its value.

Authentication Tools

Invest in some essential **authentication tools** to verify the legitimacy of your coins. A good magnifying glass can help you inspect details that are not visible to the naked eye. Additionally, consider tools like a **digital scale** for weight comparison and a **caliper** for measuring diameter. These tools can assist in identifying counterfeits.

Online Security Practices

In today's digital age, securing your online presence is just as important as protecting your physical collection. Use **strong, unique passwords** for any accounts related to coin collecting, especially auction sites and forums. Enable **two-factor authentication** wherever possible to add an extra layer of security.

Be wary of sharing too much information online. While engaging in forums and communities can be beneficial, avoid disclosing the full extent of your collection or its value. This can help prevent potential scams and theft.

Building a Network

Connecting with other collectors can provide a support system for security. Join local coin clubs or online communities to share experiences and tips on security measures. Networking with other enthusiasts can also help you stay informed about **scams** and **fraudulent activities** within the numismatic community.

Regular Audits

Conducting **regular audits** of your collection is essential. This includes checking the condition of your coins and ensuring they are stored properly. An inventory check can help you keep track of your coins and identify any discrepancies or losses. Document any changes in condition and take note of any new acquisitions.

Emergency Preparedness

Prepare for emergencies by having a **contingency plan**. This might include creating a checklist of steps to take in case of theft, fire, or natural disasters. Ensure that your family members are aware of this plan and know how to access your collection securely if needed.

In conclusion, securing your coin collection requires a multifaceted approach that combines physical, digital, and community strategies. By implementing these techniques and tools, you can protect your investment and enjoy the peace of mind that comes with knowing your collection is safe.

Legal Aspects of Coin Ownership

When it comes to coin collecting, understanding the **legal aspects of ownership** is crucial for any collector, whether you're just starting out or have been in the game for years. The laws surrounding coin ownership can vary significantly from one jurisdiction to another, so it's essential to be informed about the regulations that apply to your collection.

First and foremost, **ownership rights** are determined by the laws of your country and state. In many places, once you purchase a coin legally, you have the right to own it, sell it, or trade it. However, this can become complicated if the coin has a disputed history or is considered **culturally significant**. For instance, coins that are deemed to be national treasures may be subject to specific laws that restrict their sale or export.

Another important factor to consider is the **provenance** of your coins. Provenance refers to the history of ownership of a particular coin. Having clear documentation can protect you in case a coin you purchased turns out to be stolen or illegally obtained. It's advisable to keep records of where you acquired each coin, including receipts, appraisals, and any correspondence with previous owners or dealers.

Additionally, **tax implications** can arise from coin ownership. In many countries, coins are considered collectibles and may be subject to capital gains tax when sold for a profit. Understanding how these taxes apply to your collection is vital, especially if you plan to sell or trade coins in the future. Consulting with a tax professional who has experience in collectibles can help you navigate this aspect effectively.

It's also essential to be aware of **import and export laws**. If you plan to buy coins from international dealers or sell coins to collectors overseas, you must comply with both your country's regulations and those of the destination country. Some countries have strict laws regarding the importation of certain types of coins, especially those made from precious metals.

Furthermore, **local laws** can affect how you display and store your collection. Some municipalities have regulations regarding the display of valuable items in residential areas, especially if they are visible from the street. It's wise to check with your local authorities to ensure that your collection complies with any relevant regulations.

Lastly, consider the importance of **insurance** for your coin collection. As your collection grows in value, insuring it can provide peace of mind against theft, loss, or damage. Consult with an insurance agent who specializes in collectibles to find the right policy that covers your unique needs.In summary, being well-informed about the legal aspects of coin ownership can safeguard your investment and enhance your enjoyment of this fascinating hobby. From understanding ownership rights and provenance to navigating tax implications and insurance needs, taking the time to educate yourself can help you build a collection that not only brings joy but also stands the test of time.

15. Preserving Your Collection

When it comes to **preserving your coin collection**, the key is to create an environment that minimizes damage and maintains the integrity of your coins. Coins are sensitive to their surroundings, and even small factors can lead to deterioration. Here are some essential practices to consider.

Storage Solutions

Choosing the right storage solution is crucial. Coins should be stored in materials that do not react chemically with them. Opt for **acid-free holders**, such as coin flips, capsules, or albums specifically designed for numismatic storage. Avoid PVC holders, as they can release harmful chemicals over time.

Climate Control

The environment where you store your coins plays a significant role in their preservation. Aim for a stable temperature and humidity level. Ideally, keep your coins in a room with a temperature between **65°F and 70°F** and humidity levels around **40% to 50%**. Fluctuations can cause condensation, leading to tarnishing and corrosion.

Handling Techniques

When it comes to handling your coins, always use **clean, dry hands** or wear cotton gloves. Oils and dirt from your fingers can leave permanent marks or damage the surface of the coins. If you must pick them up, hold them by the edges to avoid touching the faces.

Cleaning Coins

Cleaning coins is a contentious topic among collectors. In general, it's best to avoid cleaning coins, as this can lead to scratches and diminish their value. If a coin is particularly dirty, consult with a professional before attempting any cleaning method. If you must clean, use **distilled water** and a soft brush, and only if absolutely necessary.

Documentation

Keeping detailed records of your collection is essential for both preservation and potential resale. Document each coin's **purchase details**, including date, price, condition, and any relevant history. This information is invaluable not only for your own reference but also for future generations.

Insurance Considerations

Consider insuring your collection, especially if it holds significant value. Speak with your insurance provider about **specialty coverage** for collectibles. This will provide peace of mind and financial protection in case of theft, loss, or damage.

Regular Inspections

Schedule regular inspections of your collection to check for any signs of deterioration or damage. Look for **tarnishing, discoloration, or signs of moisture**. Early detection can help mitigate further damage and preserve your coins for years to come.

Engaging Family

Involve your family in the preservation process. Teaching them about the importance of coin care not only helps maintain the collection but also fosters a shared appreciation for your hobby. This can create lasting memories and ensure that your passion for numismatics is passed down through generations.

Final Thoughts

Preserving your coin collection is not just about protecting your investment; it's about maintaining a legacy. By implementing these practices, you can enjoy your collection for years to come while ensuring it remains in the best possible condition for future generations to appreciate.

Proper Storage Methods

Proper storage of your coin collection is crucial for maintaining its value and ensuring its longevity. Coins are delicate items that can be easily damaged by environmental factors, improper handling, or unsuitable storage methods. Here are some essential tips to keep your coins safe and in pristine condition.

Temperature and Humidity Control

Coins should be stored in a stable environment where **temperature** and **humidity** levels are controlled. Ideally, the storage area should be kept between 65°F and 70°F (18°C to 21°C) with a relative humidity of around 30% to 50%. Excessive heat can cause coins to tarnish, while high humidity can lead to corrosion. Consider using a **dehumidifier** or an air conditioner if necessary.

Choosing the Right Storage Containers

Invest in high-quality storage containers specifically designed for coins. Options include **coin holders**, **albums**, and **slabs**. Avoid using PVC holders, as they can emit harmful chemicals that damage coins over time. Instead, look for materials like **Mylar** or **polyester**, which are safe for long-term storage. Make sure the containers are **acid-free** and **archival-safe** to prevent any chemical reactions that could harm your coins.

Handling Your Coins

When handling your coins, always make sure to do so with **clean hands** or wear **cotton gloves** to avoid leaving oils or dirt on the surface. Hold coins by the edges, never the faces, to minimize the risk of scratches or fingerprints. If you need to examine a coin closely, use a **magnifying glass** or a jeweler's loupe instead of picking it up repeatedly.

Organizing Your Collection

Keeping your collection organized makes it easier to manage and appreciate. Consider categorizing your coins by **type**, **year**, or **geographic origin**. Use a **coin inventory system** to track your collection, noting details such as purchase date, price, and any relevant history. This can be a digital spreadsheet or a dedicated software program. An organized collection not only provides a sense of accomplishment but also helps in assessing the value of your coins over time.

Regular Inspections

Conduct regular inspections of your collection to check for any signs of **damage** or **deterioration**. Look for signs of tarnish, corrosion, or any physical changes that may indicate a problem. If you notice any issues, take immediate action to address them, such as re-cleaning or re-storing the affected coins. Regular maintenance will help preserve your collection and ensure that it remains in excellent condition for years to come.

Insurance and Documentation

For high-value collections, consider obtaining **insurance** to protect your investment. Document your coins with high-quality photographs and detailed descriptions, including their condition and any relevant certificates of authenticity. This documentation will not only assist in insurance claims but also provide a record for future generations.

Storing for the Long Term

If you plan to store coins for an extended period, consider using **bank safety deposit boxes** or a **fireproof safe** at home. These options provide added security and protection against theft, fire, or water damage. Ensure that any storage location is easily accessible for you to perform regular checks.

Proper storage methods are vital for maintaining the integrity and value of your coin collection. By controlling the environment, using appropriate containers, handling coins with care, and staying organized, you can ensure that your collection remains a source of pride and joy for you and your family for generations to come.

Cleaning and Conservation Techniques

When it comes to cleaning and conserving your coin collection, the approach you take can significantly impact the value and longevity of your coins. It's crucial to remember that coins are not just collectibles; they are pieces of history that deserve careful handling and maintenance. Here are some essential techniques to ensure your coins remain in pristine condition.

Understanding the Importance of Cleaning

Many collectors grapple with the question of whether to clean their coins. While it might be tempting to make your coins shine, **cleaning can often do more harm than good**. Coins can lose their value if they are improperly cleaned, as it may remove the natural patina that contributes to their character and worth. Therefore, understanding when and how to clean is essential.

Basic Cleaning Techniques

If you decide that cleaning is necessary, start with the least invasive methods. For dirt or grime that has accumulated on the surface, **gentle rinsing with water** is often sufficient. Use distilled water instead of tap water to avoid any minerals or chemicals that could harm your coins.

For more stubborn dirt, you may use a soft brush, like a toothbrush with soft bristles. Always brush in a circular motion to avoid scratching the surface. **Never use abrasive materials** or harsh chemicals, as these can irreparably damage your coins.

Drying Your Coins

After cleaning, it's vital to dry your coins properly. Use a **soft, lint-free cloth** to gently pat them dry. Avoid rubbing, as this can create scratches. If you're concerned about moisture, consider placing the coins in a dry environment for a few hours before storing them.

Conservation Techniques

Conservation goes beyond just cleaning; it involves preserving your coins for the long term. One effective method is to store your coins in **acid-free holders** or capsules. These holders prevent exposure to air and contaminants that can cause corrosion over time.

Another important aspect of conservation is controlling the environment in which your coins are stored. Keeping them in a **climate-controlled space** will help mitigate the risks of humidity and temperature fluctuations, both of which can lead to deterioration.

Handling Your Coins

Proper handling is crucial to maintaining your coins' condition. Always hold coins by the edges to avoid transferring oils and dirt from your fingers onto the surface. If you must touch the coin, make sure your hands are clean and dry. **Wearing cotton gloves** can provide an extra layer of protection against fingerprints and smudges.

Identifying When to Seek Professional Help

Sometimes, coins may require more than just basic cleaning and conservation. If you have a particularly valuable or rare coin, consider consulting a professional conservator. They have the tools and expertise to assess the condition of your coin and recommend appropriate actions. **Professional cleaning** can help restore a coin's original beauty without risking damage.

Documenting Your Collection

Keeping a detailed record of your cleaning and conservation efforts is also beneficial. Document each coin's condition before and after cleaning, along with any treatments applied. This record can provide valuable information for future reference and can be particularly useful if you decide to sell or pass on your collection.

Final Thoughts

Cleaning and conserving your coins is not just about aesthetics; it's about preserving history. By applying the right techniques and being mindful of how you handle and store your collection, you can ensure that your coins remain valuable for years to come. Remember, **less is often more** when it comes to cleaning, and always prioritize preservation over appearance.

Insuring Your Collection

When it comes to **protecting your coin collection**, insuring it is an essential step that every serious collector should consider. Coins can represent not just monetary value but also sentimental worth, especially if they have been passed down through generations or represent significant historical moments. Having the right insurance in place can provide peace of mind, knowing that your investment is safeguarded against loss, theft, or damage.

Understanding Insurance Options

There are several types of insurance policies available for coin collections, and understanding them can help you make an informed choice. Generally, you have two main options: **homeowner's insurance** and specialized collectibles insurance.

Homeowner's insurance typically covers personal property, including coins, but the coverage may not be sufficient for high-value collections. Often, standard policies have limits on how much they will pay for collectibles, which could leave you underinsured. If you choose this route, it's crucial to review your policy and consider adding a **rider** or **endorsement** specifically for your coins to increase the coverage limit.

Specialized collectibles insurance, on the other hand, is designed specifically for items like coins, stamps, and art. These policies often provide broader coverage and may include benefits like **agreed value coverage**, which means you and the insurer agree on the value of your collection upfront. This can be particularly useful in the event of a claim, as it simplifies the process and ensures you receive a fair payout.

Determining the Value of Your Collection

Before you can insure your collection, you need to establish its value. This process typically involves **appraisal** by a qualified numismatist or appraiser who can provide an accurate assessment of your coins' worth. It's advisable to have your collection appraised regularly, especially if you acquire new pieces or if the market fluctuates significantly.

When getting an appraisal, ensure that the appraiser is **certified** and experienced in numismatics. A reputable appraiser will consider factors like **rarity**, **condition**, and **market demand** to determine the value. Keep detailed records of all appraisals, as these documents will be essential when discussing coverage with your insurance provider.

Documenting Your Collection

Proper documentation is key to ensuring that you can prove ownership and value in the event of a claim. Create a comprehensive inventory of your collection that includes:

- **Photographs** of each coin, ideally showing both the obverse and reverse sides.

- **Descriptions** that detail the coin's type, year, mint mark, and any unique features.

- **Appraisal documents** that provide evidence of value.

- **Purchase receipts** or records for each piece, which can help establish provenance.

Store this documentation in a safe place, both digitally and physically, so you can easily access it when needed.

Choosing the Right Insurer

Not all insurance companies are equipped to handle collectibles, so it's essential to choose one that specializes in this area. Look for insurers with a solid reputation in the collectibles market, and consider the following factors:

- **Coverage options** available: Ensure they offer policies tailored to coin collections.

- **Customer reviews** and ratings: Research what other collectors have experienced with the insurer.

- **Claims process**: Understand how claims are handled, including any specific requirements for filing.

- **Premium costs**: Compare quotes from different insurers, but remember that the cheapest option isn't always the best.

Maintaining Your Insurance Policy

Once your collection is insured, it's important to regularly review your policy to ensure it remains adequate. As you add new coins or if the market value changes, you may need to adjust your coverage. This could involve updating your inventory and getting new appraisals as necessary.

Additionally, stay informed about any changes in the insurance market or your insurer's policies that could impact your coverage. Regular communication with your insurance agent can help you stay on top of these details.

Protecting Your Collection Beyond Insurance

While insurance is a critical component of protecting your collection, it's also wise to take preventative measures to minimize risks. Consider implementing the following:

- **Secure storage**: Use a safe or safety deposit box to store your coins securely.

- **Environmental controls**: Ensure that your storage area is climate-controlled to prevent damage from humidity or temperature fluctuations.

- **Handling precautions**: Always handle coins with care, using gloves and avoiding direct contact with the surfaces whenever possible.

By taking these steps, you can help safeguard your collection against potential threats, ensuring that it remains a valuable asset for years to come.

Insuring your coin collection is not just a financial decision; it's a way to protect your passion and legacy. By understanding your options, documenting your collection, and maintaining open communication with your insurer, you can ensure that your investment is secure. Remember, a well-insured collection allows you to enjoy your hobby with confidence, knowing that you have taken the necessary steps to protect what you cherish.

Made in the USA
Middletown, DE
23 December 2024